Your Sun Sign as a Spiritual Guide

Your Sun Sign *as a* Spiritual Guide

J. Donald Walters
(Kriyananda)

New Age Books

ISBN: 81-7822-049-0

First Indian Edition: 2002

Published by arrangement with
Crystal Clarity Publishers, USA

Published by
NEW AGE BOOKS
A-44 Naraina Phase I
New Delhi-110 028 (INDIA)
Email: nab@vsnl.in
Website: www.newagebooksindia.com

For Sale in South Asia Only

Printed in India
at Shri Jainendra Press
A-45 Naraina Phase-I New Delhi-110 028

This book is dedicated in fond appreciation to that unlikely reader who is patient enough to wade through its murky waters from beginning to end, bravely resisting the temptation to skip back and forth, like a child on an easter egg hunt, looking up what I have said about this friend of his and that. For several themes have been developed in these pages in such a way that, for a fuller understanding of each sign, all of the other signs should be read also, and in sequence.

Contents

Preface

In the years since 1971, when this book first appeared in print, it has enjoyed considerable success not only with the general public, but among professional astrologers and psychologists as well. What has made it outstanding among the books in its field is its emphasis on self-help. Its approach is not, "This is what you are. Learn to live with it;" — but rather, "This is what you can *do* with what you are, if you want to improve your lot in life."

The point made in these pages is that every sun sign offers its own potentials for spiritual development. None is any better or worse than any other. There are no especially "spiritual" signs, except in the sense that *each* of them offers special opportunities for those born under it to develop their own unique potentials.

J. Donald Walters, perhaps better known as Kriyananda, is an internationally known authority in the ancient wisdom of India, out of which the science of astrology was born. He is known also for his deep understanding of human nature.

An American by birth, he embraced the Eastern path in 1948, becoming a direct disciple of the great master yogi, Paramhansa Yogananda (author of the spiritual classic, ***Autobiography of a Yogi***). Swami Kriyananda thus brought many years of training and experience to the creation of this little volume.

May you benefit as greatly from it as the thousands of readers before you.

Joy to you!
The Publishers

PART I

1

Why This Book?

Why still another book on the sun signs? Isn't the market fairly awash in them already?

My reason is that I'm not so much adding my own bucketful to the flood as trying to bail enough water out of this ship to locate the rudder.

Nowhere in any book have I read a clear way out of the depressing circumstances into which Fate drove me, like a peapod in a storm, when it made me a Taurean. I'm supposed, in my Taurean earthiness, to be quite unlike those airy Geminis, or those fiery Leos, but I find we do have one thing in common: We're all stuck, rudderless, wherever Fate left us. The books tell us what we are (or are *supposed* to be); they don't take the trouble to tell us what we can do about it.

Where do we go from here? If I'm drifting helplessly somewhere north of the equator, and you're becalmed somewhere south of it, then to find the equator we must go in opposite directions. If I'm a Taurean, and you're a Leo, we may need different advice on how to go about doing something constructive with our lives and how to find a sane, middle point of balance. Instead, all we ever get from popular astrology is suggestions for accepting it as our destiny to remain just where we are. Taureans are stubborn because - well, they're Taureans, and supposed to be stubborn. No one tells them how this stubbornness may be developed from sheer bull-headedness to that kind of firm loyalty to truth that can only come from being fair and open-minded. Leos are supposed to love the limelight; no one tells them how an egotistical desire to shine before others can be transformed into a purely generous wish to enlighten.

In other words, there are different levels in the manifestation of basically similar traits. But the astrological books to which I've been exposed show a tendency to throw all the strengths and weaknesses of a sign together as if into a blanket, and then let them fall out where they will. It is difficult to get a clear picture of who is really what, when, and why. *All* Leos, for instance, are supposed to love the limelight. Yet I know any number of them who don't, in fact who seem to shun it as a bomber would searchlights during an air raid. Really to understand the different influences at work in human nature, it is necessary to realize that there are higher and lower (or perhaps a better expression would be "more and less mature") ways of responding to those influences. It is easier to understand that a way *is,* clearly, more or less mature if it is also understood that the end of human development is spiritual wisdom. A trait must be considered higher or lower according to whether it takes one closer to, or farther from, this ultimate point of soul maturity.

In ancient times, astrology was praised by the wisest of men as a divine science. Why? if all it does is tell us our "hang-ups," and when would be the most favorable time for us to take a vacation? The fact is, astrology's main purpose is to help man to chart his way out of dependence on any external influences — to become a free soul, guided only by the light of truth in his own heart. As a good general must know the lay of the land, and the relative strengths and weaknesses of his enemies and allies, so a man is helped in his journey toward final freedom if he understands something of the subtle influences that are affecting him — some adversely, others beneficially. Lacking the desire to know all those influences specifically, he will find it greatly helpful even to be aware, generally, that there *are* such subtle influences at work.

The ultimate purpose of astrology is to help man to understand that he can develop himself inwardly, so as to filter out the harmful influences, and make the best use of the beneficial ones. From understanding how the external universe affects him, he can gain greater insight into the manner in which his own, internal, universe of subtle energies affects him also. By learning to develop this inner universe, he can gradually be freed of dependence on the outer.

To study the influence of the sun signs is, as any real student of astrology knows, but the merest beginning to an understanding of this divine science. Yet it is a good beginning. It provides a few real guideposts which can be helpful to a seeker in his long search for self-knowledge.

2

Can the Planets Really Affect Us?

How is it possible for distant planets to exert any influence on human lives and destinies? A great body of evidence suggests that they do. But if indeed they do, how do they do it?

The question is not so unanswerable nowadays, when it has been found that living creatures are affected by magnetism of many kinds. Mollusks open their shells in rhythm with the moon's motion. The direction snails move is affected by the earth's polarity. Human behavior is often more erratic when the moon is full, as has been revealed by various studies of criminal and mental hospital records. A number of meteorologists have found that by consulting astrology the precision of their forecasts is definitely enhanced. Countless psychiatrists have taken to casting their patients' horoscopes for greater accuracy in their diagnoses. Recently *The Wall Street Journal* printed an article on the startling accuracy of certain predictions* of stockmarket rises and declines based on the movements of the planets. The planets affect man, not personally and deliberately, but more in the way that different people are affected by the rain. Some become gloomy and depressed; others, exhilarated; still others feel themselves somehow cleansed and purified. One person may become more peaceful; another may find himself unaccountably nervous and uneasy. The objective condition is similar in all cases. It is the human responses that differ.

The planets, similarly, exert certain magnetic influences, individually as well as in various combinations, to which people respond according to their own magnetic constitutions.

An individual's subjective make-up is always affected by objective influences in the universe, but never more so than by the influences that occur at the time of his greatest openness and susceptibility: his birth. The special combination of magnetic planetary rays that were being received at the place and at the moment of his first appearance in this life affect him more exactly than they can at any subsequent time of his life, simply because his body and

*Found in *Astro-Economics, a Study of Astrology and the Business Cycle,* by Lieutenant Commander David Williams, Llewellyn Publications, St. Paul, Minnesota, 1969.

nervous system at that time represent a relatively clean slate.* Thus, they establish to a very great extent (though not entirely) the specific magnetic pattern that will determine his unique character and destiny, and how he will react to all future astral influences.

It sounds like a very interesting, but of course fanciful, theory. The compelling argument is that it works.

Numerous cases, for example, are on record of people who have been born very close together in time and place. (In astrology, even a few minutes can make for great differences in the astral influences.) The similarities have been striking. These so-called "astral twins," usually unknown to one another, have often taken ill on the same days, married on the same days, met with similar accidents and died on the same days. Such case histories may be found in various astrological works.** To duplicate them here would only be parroting the research of others.

Astrology was more advanced as a science in ancient times than it is today. Now it is still only, in

---

*The Hindu teachings claim that man's destiny is determined on a still deeper level by his karma, or actions, of past lives, and that the time of his birth coincides with a planetary configuration that is harmonious for him. This would suggest an even greater openness to the planetary influences on the part of the newborn babe.

**One fascinating book which contains descriptions of several such cases is *Astrology: The Space Age Science,* by Joseph F. Goodavage, Parker Publishing Company, Inc., West Nyack, N.Y., 1966.

a sense, being rediscovered. It would therefore be wise to look to ancient traditions as guides to present developments.

One feature that stands out most clearly in the ancient writings is the emphasis that was placed on astrology as a guide to personal development, rather than as a mere statement of problems with no suggestion of a solution. Another feature of those writings is their emphasis on spiritual progress as the true goal of all human development. The use of astrology for purely mundane purposes was considered a lower, if still acceptable, application of this essentially divine science. Astrology in its highest form was meant to help man to reverse the indignity that was imposed upon him at his birth. As he was, at that time, the more or less helpless recipient of an impersonal combination of objective influences, so now he can *and must* develop his own magnetic power, that its influence on the world around him become even greater than that of the powerful, but distant, planets. From being an effect, he learns to become a cause. Thus, the great souls of this world are able not only to guide their own destinies, but also substantially to affect for the better the destinies of people who come, even by mental attunement, within the range of their magnetic influence. It is said in *Guru Stotra,* one of the Indian Scriptures: "Even one moment in the company of a saint can be your raft over the ocean of delusion."

3

Astrology — Ancient and Modern

When the astrology books tell you that you are a Gemini, they mean that the sun was passing through the sign Gemini at the time of your birth. Rarely is the further fact stated that, in all likelihood, the sun was *not* in the *constellation* Gemini at that time.

First of all, astrology measures out exactly thirty degrees for each of the twelve signs through which the sun and other planets must pass to complete their full 360-degree cycle of the heavens. The constellations themselves were not so neatly or conveniently spaced by the Creator. In fact, their sizes vary considerably.

Astronomers sometimes refer to these variances in an effort to discredit astrology. What they do not know is that the ancient astrologers were not, as is popularly believed, concerned with the constellations as such, but rather with general areas of steady influence radiating from certain "fixed" stars, or groups of stars, in the zodiacal belt through which the planets* must pass.

It is interesting that the ancients from whom we have derived our tradition were almost unanimously agreed on the names of the constellations. Anyone with a good imagination can make out complete images from a few fixed points of reference. Three dots forming a triangle could look like an A-frame house, an arrowhead, a woman's skirt, a Christmas tree. If, as the books tell us, the ancients named the constellations after the things they saw in them, then their consideration was purely esthetic. Such wide-spread unanimity on a purely artistic level would be inconceivable. Not one of the constellations really *looks* like the image with which it has been associated. If it was a fad among the ancient goatherds to see what they could see in different configurations of stars, one assumes that there must also have been rivalry. ("I see a fence and a tree." "Idiot! It's Belshazzar throwing a feast. Can't you see that slave girl over there passing him an engraved silver chalice? and the Nubian enter-

---

*This ancient word, meaning *wanderers* was applied to all bodies that moved in relation to the fixed pattern of distant stars. It included therefore the sun and moon. The definition of a planet as a stellar satellite is a modern innovation.

tainers dancing to wild music in front of the banquet table?") The fact that there *was* unanimity suggests that imagination was not the prime consideration.

In our times, the great Christian missionary, Frank Laubach, taught millions of illiterate people to read by drawing familiar images around the unfamiliar letters of their alphabets. It seems reasonable to suppose that the ancients, similarly, drew pictures around various star groups to suggest as simply as they could the essential influences of those groups.

As a matter of fact, this is more than an attractive theory. It is known, for example, that the ancient Hindu astrologers were concerned with only a few specific stars in each constellation, and with the particular sorts of rays emanating from these stars.

Why these stars only, when the sky is full of thousands of others, all of them, conceivably, emitting various sorts of magnetic influences? The reason is that it is these few stars, specifically, resting as they do on the zodiac, whose influences are filtered through the constantly moving screen of the planets. It is their influences, then, that determine the *changing* patterns of human destiny, as opposed to others that — like the universal wish to move about, or to provide in some way for oneself — remain more or less constant. The ancients considered each zodiacal star separately as well as in groups. It was for more general purposes that they designated the different groupings as Leo, Virgo, etc., to suggest their combined influences.

This brings us to a much more serious criticism

that is commonly leveled against modern astrology. Astronomers point out that, when astrologers talk of the different zodiacal signs, they aren't really referring to the constellations *at all,* but only to fixed degrees of distance from the vernal equinox. The designation of this vernal point as the beginning of the sign, Aries, is a pure invention. In fact — owing, astronomers tell us, to a slight wobble in the earth — the vernal point moves slowly backward through the constellations.*

The modern vernal point occurred at zero degrees Aries several centuries ago, which means that it now occurs somewhere near the beginning of Pisces, not in Aries at all. In another several centuries from now the equinox will enter the constellation Aquarius.** If the books tell you that you are a Gemini, the chances are (unless you are a late Gemini)

---

*A perfectly reasonable explanation. However, the ancient Hindu astrologers advanced another, and infinitely more fascinating, reason for this precession of the equinoxes. They said that our sun rotates around a distant dual every 24,000 years. As this rotation carries us closer to the center of our galaxy, the greater intensity of spiritual rays emanating from that center causes mankind in general to become more enlightened, spiritually and intellectually. As we move slowly away from the center, mankind gradually enters a decline until, at the farthest point, he is in what is known as a dark age. The precession of the equinoxes, according to those ancient astrologers, is due to the changing galactic scene brought on by this slow rotation around our stellar dual.

**One often hears, nowadays, that we have already entered the age of Aquarius, or are on the point of doing so. So as not to blame anyone for this mistake, let us just say that the gun is guilty of having been jumped.

that the sun on your birthday is really in Taurus. Modern astrologers have elected to stick with a fixed zodiac simply to spare themselves the trouble of changing it every year. This change is, in fact, slight. It takes, at the present rate of precession, about seventy-two years for the vernal point to shift backwards a mere one degree. But the margin of difference has increased over the centuries, and is now considerable.

When we say that a person is a Gemini, therefore, we are talking a different language from that of the ancients, who were scrupulous about keeping up with the equinoctial precession. It is not, however, an unnatural language that modern astrologers have developed, but only a different one. It is important to understand how it differs if one is to understand how it really works.

4

Solar Astrology

Astrology as it is generally known today is no longer directly related to the constellations. The *signs* of the zodiac, as they are now known (to distinguish them from the *constellations* of the zodiac), are determined by their degrees of distance from the vernal equinox. At this vernal point, on about March 21st of every year, the sun's path crosses the equator from south to north. This is to say that the earth, the axis of which tilts at an angle to our path around the sun, reaches that point in its yearly journey when the Southern and Northern Hemispheres are exposed equally to the sun's light, the sun being just then directly over the equator. From that point until about June 21st the Northern Hemisphere turns more and more toward the sun, bringing longer nights than days to the southern half of our globe.

The vernal equinox as it is now viewed is a purely solar phenomenon. In ancient astrology it was considered against a background of distant constellations, but more lately no such broad reference has been made. The vernal point is taken as zero Aries; the first thirty degrees from that point are called the sign (not the constellation) Aries; the next thirty are called Taurus; the next, Gemini; and so on. Because these signs are related only to the sun's passage over the equator, they may be called the life-cycle of the sun for the succeeding solar year: its eager beginning, its outward accomplishments, its gradual return through the cold of winter to the cycle's end. Because it is the sun's journey that defines the meanings of these signs, the planetary placements in them must be judged as if one were looking at them, so to speak, through the sun's eyes. In ancient astrology, the planets were considered individually in their relation to the constellations. In solar astrology, their very placements depend on the sun's cycle. To understand the influences of the planets in solar astrology,* we must first

---

*This system has also been called *tropical* astrology, because the sun's extreme passage north and south of the equator defines the tropics of Cancer (in the north) and Capricorn (in the south). The tropics themselves, however, have nothing intrinsic to do with this system of astrology. They simply define the sun's path, a function which they perform as meaningfully in constellational astrology. The name is therefore misleading. I have named it, rather, what it essentially is: *solar* astrology.

understand the essential influence of the sun.

The ancients related the sun's influence* to man's sense of authority. In constellational (or, as it is often called, sidereal) astrology, this would refer also to man's sense of authority from the past, to his sense of traditional values,** and above all to his particular awareness of higher, divine authority, which is to say, to his special quality of wisdom. But solar astrology, a more limited science simply because it ignores the vast universe outside our own solar system, deals with our more immediate world. The sun in this system signifies, primarily, *the way, or manner, in which a person seeks to impose his authority on the world around him.*

The position of the sun in your solar horoscope shows the outward manifestation of your sense of authority: how you seek to impose your authority on others. The sun's *actual* position relative to the constellations shows how you relate this sense of authority to more universal realities.

If, in your solar horoscope, your sun is in Aries, it will tend to make you outgoing, even aggressive in your dealings with others. But assuming you were not born toward the very end of Aries, your sun's actual sidereal position will be in the constellation

---

*Western writers often relate it to man's ego identity, but this is a static definition. As a concept, it discourages further development. As a psychological aid, it offers no hint of possibility for further progress on the part of the individual. An identity, after all, is something fixed, and probably permanent.

**In Hindu astrology, the sun represents also the native's father.

Pisces. This will mean that your *inner* sense of universal influences, of authority from above, your particular brand of inner wisdom, will be Piscean. This Piscean sense, moreover, will no longer govern so large a part of your inner nature as Aries does, in solar astrology, your outer personality, for your sense of authority will no longer be the filter through which *all* the other planets must be judged. (They will be judged each on its own merit, instead, against the background of the constellations.)

One's outward personality does determine to some extent also how one approaches deep, spiritual realities, but there are many levels of consciousness in us all. On deeper levels, most of us are very different from the face we show to the world — not because we seek to deceive others, but only because those sensitive feelings which are at home in the depths of our mental seas would not survive at the surface. They are too deep to be verbalized.

The sun's placement in your solar horoscope, then, determines the way in which you seek to impress your authority on the world around you. The other planets, in this system, must be considered as each influencing especially this *outward* manifestation of your personality.

Your moon's placement reflects the *attitude* (as distinct from the way, or manner) with which you seek to impress your authority on others.

Your Mars indicates the quality of energy with which you seek to impress your authority.

Your Mercury determines the intellectual filter through which you impress your authority — not the quality of your intelligence so much as the general direction that it takes.

Your Venus indicates the kind of sensitivity with which you seek to impress yourself on others — in artistic and love matters as well as in your work.

The sun, moon, Mars, Mercury, and Venus — the inner circle, in other words, of our solar family, and the closest of them to your earth — represent your more intimate, personal nature. The outer planets represent more impersonal influences on your nature.

Jupiter's placement in a solar horoscope indicates a person's expansive quality — whether, for example, he is altruistic, philosophical, fame-loving, or self-indulgent.

Saturn represents the counteractive influence. It affects one's capacity for getting things together, for concentration on self-discipline, or, in a negative sense, one's inhibitions and sense of restriction.

In relatively recent years, three more planets have been discovered: Uranus (in 1781), Neptune (in 1846), and Pluto (in 1930). There is some evidence in ancient mythologies that these planets may once have been known. There is also a considerable body of evidence that certain ancient civilizations may have possessed the necessary technological advancement to be capable of observing these planets. In what has survived to us of ancient astrology, however, no mention is made of any planets beyond Saturn, though a few Hindu works refer obscurely to a planet, Mandi, that seems later to have been lost sight of. With the help of references in ancient mythology, and more especially by an empirical study of people's lives as they seem to be affected by the natal placements and temporal transits of these planets, astrologers have generally agreed on some of their effects.

Uranus may be taken to indicate the originality, or initiative, with which one seeks to impress his authority on the world.

Neptune in the different signs indicates the channel of expression for what might be called one's psychic sensitivity (whether genuine, or merely emotional and delusive) in one's work and human relationships.

Pluto, the outermost planet of the solar system, was so recently discovered that astrologers are still guessing about the nature of its influence. There seems to be a growing consensus, however, that it indicates the channel by which a person seeks regeneration — perhaps after failure and disappointment, or after repression and confinement.

It must be noted, however, that Neptune and Pluto especially, and Uranus to some extent, move so slowly through the zodiac as to submit whole generations to the same sign-influences. From this it may be inferred that these outer planets are too general in their influences to be deeply meaningful by sign alone in an individual's horoscope, though more personal meanings can indeed be drawn from their placement in the houses* and from their aspects** to the other planets. (In fact, it is possible that by these aspects some compensation has been made in recent years for the failure of solar astrology

*The departments of life as they are revealed in a horoscope.
**The relative positions of the planets to one another.

to relate the planets to the more distant stars.)

It would be interesting to see whether accurate astrological systems could be developed by using for a basis one or another of the planets instead of the sun. If Mars, for example, could be made the foundation for such a system, then instead of Mars determining the quality of energy with which one seeks to impress his authority on the world, the sun, rather, would indicate the particular kind of confidence with which he directs his energies — a shift of emphasis from the outward effects of one's efforts to the quality of the efforts themselves.* But such a system would probably have to be developed by a different civilization from our own.

In fact, one cannot but note, in this context, that Western astrology is a natural outgrowth of Western society, where man is exceptionally goal-oriented, where the traditional emphasis is on conquering nature rather than harmonizing oneself with it, and where chief importance is placed on the individual — not as he relates to his inner world or to universal realities, but rather as he relates to, and can stand in personal dignity before, his fellowman. Personality, not the eternal soul, has been the common concern of Western man. It has become more and more so, interestingly enough, the farther the sun signs have become separated, by equinoctial precession, from the constellations.

It is interesting to note, also, that the growing interest of Western astrologers in constellational

---

*One is reminded here of the basic precept of Karma yoga: "action without desire for the fruits of action."

astrology coincides with a growing interest, in the West, in the ancient philosophies of the East. Man's relationship to the universe is the special concern of those philosophies. It is in the East, also, where constellational astrology still continues to be practiced.

One reason Western astrologers are turning increasingly to the constellational system is that they are discovering, as their own mental horizons expand, that their system is too limited. A comparison might be drawn here to the straight lines on a map, which serve well enough so long as we are concerned only with small areas, but which give a distorted picture for larger areas of our globe. Solar astrology serves well enough if all we concern ourselves with is human personality, and particularly with that aspect of personality which concerns our efforts to relate significantly to (in other words, to impress our authority upon) the world around us. But once our own view of life broadens, discrepancies begin to appear, and Western astrologers have found these discrepancies bewildering — until they turned for help to constellational astrology.

In predicting the future, for example, solar astrology is accurate primarily insofar as the future is determined for us by our own personalities. But people are becoming aware that there are deeper influences at work within us — subconscious impulses, old karmic debts and credits — that never rise so close to the surface as to become identified with our outward personalities. Western astrologers, unfamiliar with these influences, yet growingly aware that such influences do exist, are beginning to feel cramped by a science that, in confining them to such a small segment of our galaxy — the solar system — succeeds also in limiting their understanding. (For it is unfortunately true that, while the growth of our understanding is at first facilitated by the intellectual systems which we build for ourselves, later, after we reach a certain point in our development, those very systems become a hindrance to the growth of further understanding.) In making predictions, they find themselves forced constantly to "hedge their bets," or else to explain themselves hastily afterwards. (Some of them simply leave town!) Nowhere among solar astrologers does one encounter the amazing accuracy of that Hindu astrologer, for example, who, when Jawaharlal Nehru (India's late prime minister) was still a boy, predicted from his horoscope that he would someday become "the maharaja of all maharajas" in India. But accuracy among *good* Hindu astrologers is no novelty.

We are dealing, then, in this booklet with a more objective and superficial system, named solar astrology, and specifically with the starting point of this system, the sun signs. What I have done is seek to explore these familiar sun signs in order to see how they can be related to the broader, more ancient, insights out of which they have grown. Instead of writing yet another analysis of how people, born under the different signs, act and react with the world around them, I have sought to show how their personalities (so important to them, as Westerners!) can be used to help them — to help *you* — to develop a more universal awareness.

5

Astrology as a Mystical Science

Lives there a person so bound to belly needs as never to have looked up at night to the stars, and pondered, if only fleetingly, their awesome distance and mystery? One of man's commonest poetic flights is to contemplate this vastness in relation to his own littleness, and the unimaginable spans of cosmic time in comparison to these few brief minutes of life with which we seek to crowd eternity.

But if anyone will lift more than a quick eye to the heavens, and will lie down somewhere alone instead, and gaze long and deeply up at the stars, a new and deeper understanding may come to him.

At first, communing with the infinite mystery of

creation, he will sense his own almost laughable insignificance. That, however, which is truly insignificant may as well be ignored. Our thoughtful stargazer, once reaching this point of self-forgetfulness in the contemplation of realities too vast for any other consideration, may begin subtly to identify his consciousness with those realities — to feel that in some way he and they are intimately related.

At this point he may recoil, as if from the brink of insanity. Shaken back to his "normal" worldly self, he will remind himself with wry amusement that he still has the grocery bill to pay, and the car to get serviced.

But supposing he braved this fear of insanity, and climbed out of his daily rut long enough to contemplate seriously the possibility of a grander identity? He might realize, then, that somehow, out of that vast mystery, we have all come. We are allied to it. Nor are we merely its products: When our few lines on this little wayside stage have been spoken, we shall return to that mystery. It is, in the greater sense, our *only* reality. The atoms of our bodies, the feelings and thoughts that make up our awareness — all, all are real only as manifestations of that infinite wonder, whatever it might be.

One of the higher purposes of astrology is to help man to become more aware of the subtle cord of unity by which all things are bound, all as parts of a whole, all real only in the sense that the whole is real. Astrology seeks to demonstrate some of the subtle interrelationships that exist between the objective universe and individual man. By increasing his awareness of cosmic influences, astrology seeks to awaken in man a sensitivity to the presence of similar responses in himself, like the sympathetic vibrations of open strings on a piano, without which those external influences would have no effect, and would simply pass him by. Discovering these deeper levels of response within himself, man can then learn to use them deliberately, and to emancipate himself from any cosmic dictate that he doesn't choose to accept.

By plunging deeper into his own nature, man discovers not only his basic identity with universal realities, but also still deeper levels within himself where he can actually *divorce* himself from those realities, remaining aloof from them as if he were, indeed, greater than they.

But how can man, a mere product of this universe, claim to be greater than it is? In size, of course he is not. His greatness lies in his discovery of levels of reality where universal laws no longer hold sway, because *they are themselves but the products of that reality.* To discover on deepest levels who and what we are is to discover, literally, what the universe is, for we and it are both the manifestations of that same truth. Though sages have spoken of it by different names, they have recognized it as one: the still Ocean of Consciousness out of which all the waves of creation have appeared.

The highest purpose of astrology is to assist man on this inward journey. The true goal, then, of astrology is not to fascinate people with endless proofs of their subtle kinship to this universe, but to take them from outward theory to inward practices. This is the science of yoga, known since ancient times in India as the science of *inner* astrology.

But other cultures have been no strangers to this highest search. It is what Christians, among others, know as the search for God.

6

Meditations on the Sun Signs

The first and most obvious feature of the zodiac is that it forms a complete circle.

One may think that this circle is manifestly unrealistic. It treats the planets and the sun as if they, like our moon, were revolving around our earth. A number of astrologers, indeed, acting on the assumption that their early predecessors were simply ignorant of the astronomical facts, have been urging the adoption of a heliocentric system of astrology.

Yet, once the constellations, too, are included in our reckoning, it seems obvious that the sun won't do for a center, either.

Or will it? or will even our earth?

We are faced with a fascinating paradox. If, as science tells us, there is no fixed center anywhere in the universe to which everything else can be related, then *any* point may be taken for a center as well as any other. For in this case a center, as a useful concept, becomes only a reference point, not a universal objective reality. We can begin our search for reality at any point, expanding outward from there ultimately to include the whole. That (partly at least) is why the Hindu scriptures say, "The Spirit is center everywhere, circumference nowhere."

And why a Hindu sage, when told by a Western visitor that she had traveled a great distance to see him, replied: "You did not travel at all. From your own reference point, you are the center of all things. It is they which move, not you, when you change their scenery."

A difficult thought, perhaps? Yet surely an eminently practical one when we consider the zodiac. For, regardless of how the planets move relative to one another, it is how their rays converge on our earth that concerns us when we cast a horoscope. Indeed, astrology is not only geocentric: It takes for its focal point the very individual who is under consideration.

In a circle there can be no real beginnings and endings, no question of absolute progression *from* one point *to* another, as there is in a straight line. In a circle, if one goes far enough in either direction he ends up where he began. Indeed, there is not even any question of really ending. The terminus of one sequence is but the starting point of another.

Man likes to think in terms of starts and finishes,

of fixed centers and fixed boundaries. It suits his finite mind to tie things up neatly — to tell a story, and then to put it forever into its little box with the statement, "And they lived happily (or sorrowfully, or successfully, or in frustration or anger) ever afterward." It pleases him — perhaps only because, having but one set of vocal cords, he can sing only one song at a time — to think of progress as a movement in one direction only — a straight line that admits of no returns.

But human thinking is beginning to outgrow the old straight-line, fixed boundary, Euclidean-style concept of life and of the universe. Mankind generally is becoming more aware, too, that in every facet of life the whole is implied, that opposites are not so far apart as was once thought, that goals are where *we* choose to place them, and not placed by Cosmic Law at set points on some universal, objective journey.

The signs of the zodiac, then, represent in a sense an arbitrary beginning, and no real ending at all. Implicit in each of the signs are, in a subtle but actual sense, all of the others. They represent, not categorical differences from one another, but only different emphases — like the various sizes of waves on a single body of water.

Men used to speak confidently of East and West. But when Western culture went far enough westward, it discovered that it was now *east*, not west, of the so-called Orient. People, similarly, are sometimes tempted to see one zodiacal sign as more advanced than another, but the finish of every cycle is only the prelude to a new one. Every sign, in fact, has its saints and its sinners, and none has more of either than any other.

Springtime has been selected as the starting point of the zodiac, perhaps because we associate its moods with fresh beginnings. The fiery eagerness that is Aries — the first of the zodiacal signs — suggests youth, uncontrol, inexperience. Yet it can also mark the renewed aspirations of a wise man who, after a lifetime of tears shed over the pains of life, learns at last with a calm mind to accept reality as it is, and discovers with this acceptance that he can now build once again in a spirit of hope. Aries marks not only the enthusiasms of youth, but also those of progressively deeper levels of maturity — the sense of cleanness that follows a long siege of rain, the purification and forgiveness that can come only to one who has known sin.

There is indeed in the zodiac a sort of going out and coming in again, like a pardoned prodigal son, wiser and better for one's fling, ready to set out ever and again on new rounds of adventure and learning.

There is also the final lesson to be learned that one can learn nothing final from these repeated goings and comings, these constantly changing involvements and disillusionments, from the ups and downs and ins and outs of a relative existence. As there is no end to a circle, so no end is ever reached by the person who thinks, "Let me do this, that, and the other thing, and *then* at last I shall taste perfect fulfillment." Every fulfillment carries with it already the seeds of some fresh disappointment. The way to real progress must be understood, finally, to lie not in the unending turnings of the wheel, but in seeking the point of rest at the center — that calm, divine point in one's Self of which all of the signs are expressions, and which is yet defined by (and therefore limited by) none of them.

The sun crosses the equator at the vernal equinox on about March 21st. For the next six months it is in the Northern Hemisphere, reaching a zenith at the summer solstice on about June 21st. At the autumnal equinox (September 23rd) it again crosses the equator, and spends the next six months in the Southern Hemisphere, reaching what for us in the north is a nadir on about December 22nd, the winter solstice.

This cyclic journey provides some interesting food for thought.

It seems evident that there is a subtle overall difference between the first six signs and the last.* There is in the first six a sort of "going out"; in the second, a "coming back." The passage of the sun into the Northern Hemisphere, bringing as it does to the north longer days than nights, may be associated with a more daytime mood. The signs that correspond with the six months when the Northern Hemisphere tilts away from the sun correspond to a more nocturnal mood.

One might even relate the signs to the hours of the day, giving them two hours each. Starting at 6 a.m., the mood of Aries corresponds to the hours of 6

*My observations might have to be altered by a close observation of the effects of the signs on people of the Southern Hemisphere, effects with which I am not sufficiently familiar.

— 8 o'clock. (To associate these hours with Aries, one must struggle bravely to imagine a healthy, vigorous person who has slept well and can't wait to leap out of bed to greet a new day!) Taurus, then, would correspond to the hours of 8 — 10 a.m., when one sets out with vigor and enthusiasm to get a grip on the tasks facing him this day. (Most writers miss the considerable capacity for enthusiasm that is a hallmark of the Taurean nature.) 10 a.m. to noon is, ideally, a time of quickening interest in the problems at hand, with perhaps a scattering of one's forces in his growing awareness of the sheer number of those problems. Gemini's influence is symbolized here.

The afternoon is a time for greater seriousness. The tenacity of Cancer is seen from noon to 2 p.m., with its capacity for "homing in" on the issues that it has decided are important, and letting the others float by untouched. The Leonine dignity and loyalty, serenely at home in the work to which it has committed itself for that day, fits well the hours of 2 - 4 p.m. (Interestingly, since Leo is the sun's own sign, these are also, in warm weather, the warmest hours of the day.) 4 - 6 p.m. is a time for winding up the little details of the day's activities — excellently suited to Virgo's meticulous influence.

Libra (6 - 8 p.m.) coincides with a time for relaxed personal enjoyment in the peace of one's own home. 8 - 10 p.m. is, in keeping with Scorpio's influence, a good time for thinking of one's own inner life, for gathering his forces back into himself so that, when he dives into outward activity again the following day, it will be from his inner self, not as a mere puppet of the influences in his surounding environment. 10 p.m. to midnight is a time to prepare the pleasant surrender of all cares into the arms of sleep. Sagittarius, carefree and friendly, yet curiously uninvolved, aspiring happily (never grimly) to the heights, may well be said to fit the mood of this time of night.

The regathering of one's forces (this time with a heavier, more "no-nonsense" intent than under Scorpio's influence — as if to cut sharply thought the vain follies of the day) expresses both the early hours of sleep from midnight to 2 a.m., and the concentrative, focalizing power that is Capricorn.

If one's sleep is deep there occurs somewhere in the middle part of the night (symbolized by the hours of 2 - 4 a.m.) a gradual dissolution of the petty sense of ego. This soul expansion fits well with the impersonal, expansive quality of Aquarius.

The all-penetrating expansion of Pisces, welling up as it does from inner depths, and reaching out in sympathy to the surrounding world, is well exemplified by the hours of 4 - 6 a.m. The psyche now begins its climb out of the depths of impersonal sleep and, reaching out gradually to the world again, prepares itself for the sudden, enthusiastic awakening that is Aries: 6 a.m., and the start of a new day.

Interestingly, at the time of the vernal equinox the hours I have assigned to each sign will actually coincide with the appearance of that sign on the eastern horizon.

A curious fact is the affinity that exists between opposite signs of the zodiac, the "day" signs being more externally directed; the "night" signs, more internally directed. (One is put in mind here of the tides that swell simultaneously on opposite sides of the earth under the pull of the moon's gravity.) Aries, with its fiery, outgoing enthusiasm, matches Libra, with its complementary wish to bring things to a peaceful balance, yet its peculiar tendency to rush to extremes in its frantic efforts to correct its imbalances! Taurus, directing its great drive outwardly, is complemented by its opposite, Scorpio, the sign of *inner* power. What astrology "buff" has not observed with a smile the twin enthusiasms of Gemini and Sagittarius: the one mental, preoccupied with specific things and specific ideas; the other more general, more idealized, an enthusiasm for enthusiasm itself rather than for any specific objects? The concentration of Cancer on matters of personal concern is offset (even, in a sense, rebuked) by the concentration of Capricorn on larger, often impersonal, issues. Leo and Aquarius both seek to uplift, to enlighten, but Leo does so more often with the sense that he himself is the center of whatever good that he is doing, whereas Aquarius rises swiftly above such personal considerations, concentrating on the broader picture: the benefits that are to be received from him by others. Virgo and Pisces, finally, both tend to enter through the fine seams of life, but Virgo does so by its preoccupation with fine details, whereas Pisces does so from a wish to expand, to enter into life in all its myriad expressions, to become one with the universe.

This view of "outward" and "inward" signs does not contradict the earlier claim that no sign is more advanced or more spiritual than any other, for the outward focus of the "day" signs may be the gift of wisdom, gathered through many lives of inward seeking. Wisest and best of men, indeed, is he who has gathered and learned to manifest in himself the lessons that are to be found in all of the signs.

We may pause, finally, to reflect on a point that is of vital importance to self-understanding through the sun signs. It is that in the weaknesses of each sign lie also its particular strengths. This is to say that the very faults which now paralyze us can, in their own higher octaves, be our very passport to perfection. The opposite also is true, of course, if one is seeking ways of compounding his mistakes, but our concern here is with how to rise out of delusion, not with how to fall into it more deeply than ever.

Astrology offers, if nothing else, fascinating and deep insights into certain universal realities of human nature. For this reason alone, if for no other, it is worthy of study even by "dedicated" non-believers.

PART II

1

Your Sun Sign and You

As you read the following descriptions of the sun signs, you should be able to recognize something of yourself in all of them. If you do not, it will mean either that I have failed in my attempt to be completely clear in my exposition, or that your own life would be enriched if you developed it more deeply in one or more of its key departments. For essentially what the signs depict, segment by segment, is the Complete Man.

If, on the other hand, you feel that your own sun sign does not fit you *better* than any other sign, it could mean that your own sense of authority (determined by the sun's influence) is not as fully developed as it might be, and that you find it difficult to *project* your true inner nature. Your horoscope would suggest reasons for this difficulty, which may or may not be a fault in your character depending on how fully you yourself need to relate to the world around you. Most probably, if your nature is more receptive than outgoing, or if you live more on a level of subjective impressions and quick, spontaneous reactions than of deep or deliberate response to life's challenges, it is your rising sign whose influence will be the most evident in your personality. If, on the other hand, you are deeply introverted, or if what life really means to you, personally, is more important to you than how you deal with it (this need not necessarily denote introversion), it is your moon's influence that will very likely predominate.

I have divided the descriptions for each sign into two parts: the essential influence of the sign itself, and what it means when the sun is posited in that sign. You will gain fuller self-understanding if you consider your rising sign (the sign that was rising on the eastern horizon at the time of your birth), your moon, and each of your planets in connection with the signs. Visualize the separate influence of each as if it were acting as a filter for the sign it occupies. For a quick view of the salient features in your personality, the most important considerations are your rising sign, your moon, and your sun.

It is your rising sign alone that determines the "houses," or particular areas in your life, in which you are especially receptive to the various planetary rays. Your rising sign, therefore, suggests also your basic *quality of receptivity* — how things impress you, how you tend to view things. If, for example, your rising sign is Gemini, the impressions you receive from the world around you will have a distinctly Geminian, or mental, cast to them. Insofar as they do not call for a *strong* response from you (which would call into play your sun nature), your quick reactions, too — those which come "off the top of your head" — will be Geminian.

Your moon indicates your personal attitudes: what values you attach to things, people and situations — what they *mean* to you, personally. If, for example, your moon is in Leo, all those Geminian impressions you receive may take on special meaning and interest for you only if you can see how they might help you to share your light, in the form of new insights, with others.

Your sun, as I have already said, indicates the way in which you seek to impress your authority on others. If, then, your sun is in Taurus, your inner desire to share with others (suggested by the fact that your moon is in Leo) will find its outward expression through steady, determined, and persistent effort, quite possibly in artistic ways (because Taurus loves beauty), and will be strongly colored by the kind of abstract, Geminian ideas in which terms you yourself see the world.

Your rising sign more often than not will determine your superficial reactions — those which spring only from your impressions, rather than from your deep inner feelings. To absorb an impression, your moon must give it personal meaning for you; if it does not, the impression remains superficial. If, after absorbing an impression, it also becomes personally meaningful for you to respond to it, then the way in which you respond will be determined chiefly by your sun sign.

The positions in your solar horoscope relate particularly to your nature as it has developed in your contacts with the world of men. Because that world has been, in all probability, very important in your life, your sun nature marks your most likely natural point of departure in your spiritual search. But the more you develop an inner, spiritual life of your own, by daily meditation, the more meaningful all these influences will be to you in their actual, constellational positions.

2

ARIES

March 21 - April 19

The Sign

Aries is the vigorous first thrust in a season of youthful beginnings. The exuberance of springtime — reflected in all three of the spring signs — is allied to those periods in the ego's development when it reaches out to life in hope and expectation, with that strange blend of self-involvement and self-forgetfulness which one finds in a child. It is a period when one's own interests seem all-absorbing, leaving room for but vague recognition of anything or anyone else — a sign, not necessarily of insensitivity or egotism, but sometimes rather of that perfect concentration of energy which alone leads to the highest kinds of success.

The mood of Aries, the first of the spring signs, is

more than a one-time thing in our lives, and in the soul's long journey toward perfection. It is also that mood of relief and new beginnings which comes after great tests have been passed, or difficult lessons at last have been learned. It is a mood of recognition that, in the "evernow-ness" of eternity, there can always be forgiveness — and a chance to make amends. It may, then, also be a season for calling out to all men with brotherly love: "See, I've found a way out of our age-old predicaments! Join me in this new adventure, and soon we'll all be free!" It may be a season for wise and deeply concerned saints, as well as for self-preoccupied and callous egotists.

Aries is ruled by Mars, the planet of energy. The fact that Aries is the sign of the Ram suggests the way in which it directs Mars' energy. For a ram, when fighting, relies on a series of hard butts to win its battles, charging each time as if to win everything in a single, terrible impact.

The influence of Aries is aptly suggested by the dynamic energy of fire. Aries, the first of three fire signs, is akin to the first burst of flames when the paper and kindling of a bonfire have been lit.

The key to the influence of this sign is *starting energy*.

The Sun in Aries

If your sun is in Aries, your way of externalizing your own sense of authority is to get things started. You are a born trailblazer, probably bold, energetic, and ambitious. Since most people are timid about taking that first necessary step themselves, once *you* have taken it you may find others trailing along after you. Your natural initiative is one of the ingredients of true leadership.

A pioneer's path is no safe or well-traveled highway. The innovator must be willing to make mistakes and bear the consequences. Your willingness to do so may mark you for the sort of person who, before he rushes into something, forgets to check whether there are any angels treading about. But it may also mark you for one who lives *intelligently* by the motto, "Nothing ventured, nothing gained," or even for a wise man who looks upon success and failure with indifference, measuring the merit of an undertaking in terms of the lessons to be learned from it. In any case, the secret of your courage will be the blessed conviction that, no matter how many disasters may beset you, you can always start again. Like your symbol, the Ram, you can win prolonged struggles only by a series of repeated, vigorous thrusts of the kind that most people associate with energetic beginnings. There can be no undertaking too great for you, if you approach it enthusiastically each day as if it were for the first time.

All of us have, or should have for our own progress on all levels of life, something of this Aries quality in us. The depressing suggestion of irrevocability that attends every failure, every misfortune, can be dismissed in an instant once one learns to say, "But that belongs to the past. From this moment onward my life will improve!" Success and failure are necessary and inextricable parts of worldly existence, but the soul of man is eternal, unchanging, unaffected by any outward ups and downs. The more we learn to live *from within*, the better we know that there is no past and future; there is only *now*, and every moment can become our long-sought doorway to eternal freedom. As Swami Sri Yukteswar said, "Forget the past. The vanished lives of all men are dark with many shames. Human conduct is ever unreliable until man is anchored in the Divine. Everything in future will improve if you are making a spiritual effort now."* The Spirit is ever new. Every breath that one takes is a psychological opportunity to make a fresh beginning in our lives. This is the mood of Aries. Some room is needed for it in the life of every man.

Every human quality, no matter how universally needed, has its pitfalls. In every strength, its opposite weakness is implied. Aries, the sign of starting energy, leaves to other signs such necessary additional virtues as patience, plodding persistence, dogged determination. Aries natives who lack a balancing influence from other signs are continually amusing (or exasperating) their friends by the complete predictability with which they apply themselves to every undertaking: the blazing beginning that peters out somewhere around the first corner. Aries gets other people all fired up to join him in a venture, then (perhaps after a week) wonders what they are doing still plodding along on that "old" project, when he himself has discovered something really exciting and new. Aries needs the kind of

---

**Autobiography of a Yogi*, by Paramhansa Yogananda, Self-Realization Fellowship, Los Angeles, California, p. 122.

work in which every day brings him new challenges, new opportunities to make an eager beginning. But too great an eagerness only to start things may result in actually starting nothing. The Aries native who spreads his energies too thin only fritters them away; people gradually see through his thin veneer of self-confidence, and cease believing in his grandiose schemes. Such a person is like one who wants to start a bonfire with only one newspaper, and, to ensure a very large fire as soon as possible, spreads the paper over a broad area. He puts a lighted match first here, then there, then in another place, each time expecting the first encouraging flames from the paper to leap up into a huge conflagration; and each time getting — nothing. He may feel suffocated by the word *patience,* but he does need to learn *control.* A little energy carefully focused can accomplish more than a great deal scattered in every direction. Even one or two pages from that newspaper, carefully crumpled and inserted judiciously at one place, might easily ignite the whole bonfire.

Aries doesn't usually like to think too far ahead, unless he can include somewhere in his schemes the prospect of a fresh start. His friends in other signs may wish he were more of a cautious planner; indeed, to master his own line of work he may need to balance his starting enthusiasms with a more distant vision. But real progress for him consists in exploring on deeper levels his own natural ability to live fully *here* and *now.*

In a worldly sense, to live only in the present is a mark of youthful immaturity. But in his callow beginnings man often reveals at least the germ of ripe understanding.

It is the mark of spiritual wisdom, also, to be able to live fully in the present. The difference is that the true sage lives *in,* not *for,* the moment. Thus, he lives in eternity. Aries, in his tendency to seize the joy of the moment, has only to go a step deeper to realize that "ever-new joy" which springs from within, and which is the mark of soul-consciousness.

There are currents of energy in the spine which flow in rhythm with the currents of man's consciousness. The upward movement of energy is associated with awakening, with life-affirmation and enthusiasm. To bring this energy upward in the spine helps correspondingly to lift one's spirits. Aries relates naturally to this upward flow; Aries natives should stimulate it consciously by various breathing exercises of yoga, by meditation, by selfless service, and by constant and eager self-offering to the Divine. If instead they allow most of the energy to flow downward, they may not only scatter their forces, but even develop the most negative traits of their sign: bossiness, and a demanding, quarrelsome, and dictatorial nature. All of these negative traits can to a great extent be transformed by simply directing the energy upward in the spine to the brain, the spiritual seat in the body.

This upward flow is subtly associated with the inhalation; it can actually be stimulated by a deliberate, slow intake of breath. Try inhaling moderately slowly, and simultaneously bring the energy of your body upward through the spine. Accompany this upward movement with a mental affirmation of life and inner awakening. Focus breath and energy at the point between the eyebrows for as long as you can hold your breath *comfortably,* and feel that all discouragement, fear and other negative qualities are being burned up in the blaze of inner power that you have generated. As you exhale again, feel that you are throwing out of your system the last poisonous fumes of negativity. Repeat this process several times.

Then meditate calmly, allowing the radiant inner sun at the point between the eyebrows (the seat of spiritual vision) completely to absorb you in an awareness of the Timeless Now.

Remember, every moment in life is an opportunity for rededication to the highest quest, the spiritual. Aries can go far if, casting off the hypnosis of every failure, he can learn to see the long journey of life as an unbroken series of ever-fresh beginnings.

> "With the first love of true lovers, teach me to love Thee."
>
> — *Paramhansa Yogananda*

3

Taurus

April 20 - May 20

The Sign

Taurus is the first of the earth signs, and the second of the spring signs. A good symbol for this month is the fresh earth in springtime: soft and rich, ready to produce an abundance of beautiful flowers and useful vegetation. Beauty (because Taurus is ruled by Venus) and usefulness (because Taurus is an earth sign, and also what is known as a *fixed* sign) are two principal concerns of this zodiacal position; happy is the Taurean native who can bring their apparent opposition into harmonious balance — who can learn to see beauty in usefulness and usefulness in beauty.

Taurus represents that time of the year when the seeds, having already been planted, now begin to send shoots up out of the ground, each eagerly claiming its own place in the sun. It is a season of slow, quiet beginnings, of great patience in preparation, but of remarkable vigor for growth once a start has been truly made.

Taurus is the sign of the Bull. Writers have made much of this symbol; especially they point out the uncontrollable rage of bulls when provoked. Yet in the Orient, where the astrological sign-symbols originated, these animals are docile creatures, not feared at all, often to be seen driven through the streets to pasture by small children. In the Orient the bull symbolizes, rather, the capacity to persist steadfastly in any determined direction — like a bull pulling a plow, straining only the harder whenever the plow encounters resistance in the soil.

Taurus stands for the spirit of "taking hold," of carrying through to completion whatever has once been started, of *sustaining energy.*

The Sun in Taurus

If your sun is in Taurus, you seek to express your sense of authority by getting a firm grip on life. Where Aries likes to see life as a continuous series of ever-new beginnings, you prefer to see even beginnings as preserving a kind of overall continuity. Even if, like several famous Taureans, you favor revolution, you seek your justification for it in the perpetuation of some nobler tradition. Whereas the spirit of Aries may spark sudden, brilliant beginnings, more often than not it is the spirit of Taurus which is needed to carry a work — especially a difficult work — through to completion. For it takes a certain dogged persistence, typified by this sign, to be able to plow steadily forward through life no matter what the obstacles to fulfillment.

On the highest levels, Taurus aids in the development of *nishtha,* steadfastness to one's spiritual goals. But Taureans who are not developed enough to receive these influences on the higher levels of their being may manifest them in more worldly ways. Many Taureans express their solar nature in a desire to set, or "fix," things in their environment, to control their world and rule out the unpredictable from their lives as much as possible. Security is important to every Taurean, but not so much, necessarily, the security of personal ownership as of assured continuity. For a Taurean, this need for continuity can be more a question of abstract principle than of personal possession, though it translates as ownership if the native himself lives on a level of egoic desires. The Taurean needs the secure knowledge that he always has a solid base from which to work. This base may be a home of his own, or only a firm understanding on which all his further investigations can be built.

If your sun is in Taurus, your power and drive are considerable. Your need occasionally to recuperate them is, therefore, also considerable. (Hence also your probable need for a home base where you can rest securely after heavy labors.) Because of your friendly and often gentle manner (allied to your Venus-inspired love of beauty and harmony), and because you are often slow to get started in things, people tend to underestimate the phenomenal vigor that you can bring to bear on any project once you take it up, or the unflagging drive with which you can carry it through to completion. Once you take up a work, you will stay with it when everyone else is ready to drop from exhaustion. Once you really take up a cause, let us hope it is the right one, else you will probably hang onto it until the ship sinks. You are like the mushroom, which, though soft and yielding, is capable as it grows of breaking its way up through a slab of concrete by its steady, unrelenting application of pressure.

What is the mainspring of your great energy? Many people assume that it is simply a love for hard work. Surprisingly perhaps, that is not the case. In fact, there are many Taureans who avoid work quite as zealously as others embrace it, who even throw their energies in true Taurean fashion into various forms of self-indulgence. In every Taurean, moreover, ruled as he is by Venus, there probably exists a deep, instinctive love of ease.

But ask yourself: Why is it so necessary for you to feel that you *must* get a grip on things? Why do so many Taureans feel that they must establish their world in set patterns, and in everything try to rule out the unpredictable? Someone who is sure of his grip doesn't need to make an issue of getting one. That, in fact, is the real secret of the famous Taurean drive. The Taurean is *not* sure.

Taurus is a springtime mood. The young, tender shoots that first show their heads above the ground would be aware, if they thought about it at all, how great are the odds against their survival. Hungry animals, sudden frost, excessive heat: Young shoots, for all their vigorous growth, are much more vulnerable to disaster than their cousins, the trees. Their strength lies in their own zeal for growth. (How quickly a baby shoot "shoots up" to become a large plant!) It lies in their ability to be beaten to the ground — only to rise again and again in hope, with renewed determination to keep right on growing to maturity.

Taurus is essentially a young sign; it possesses both the exuberance and the vulnerability of youth. Intent, like the tender shoots, on making a place for itself in the sun, it is yet, like them, easily hurt — albeit, again like them, not easily discouraged. What passes in others' eyes for self-confidence is usually only eagerness, a drive for accomplishment that is the more vigorous because, in fact, it considers the odds against success to be so great.

Doubt, not confidence, nor even a love of hard work, is the goad which drives the Taurean to ever-greater determination in his efforts to set things so that *nothing* can go wrong. This is the self-doubt of one who is still young and untried. Amusingly, perhaps, the Taurean feels that his capabilities have not yet been truly tried even after he reaches old age. Self-doubt drives him ever to prove himself to himself again and again.

If you are a Taurean, your very wish to set things permanently around you is born of an inner uncertainty as to what might happen if you didn't, if you allowed things to get out of hand. It is the anxiety of the young shoot, fearing that it may not yet be strong enough to take the world's punishments, anxious to prove that it can.

There are, of course, some of these Taurean traits in all of us. Whenever you, whatever your sun sign, become *too* anxious to get a firm grip on things, try to remember that the source of your anxiety rests not so much in the unreliability of things in themselves as in your own *inner* security. It is the earth element in us that makes us want things always to be rock-firm. Our earth itself, however, is a madly spinning ball. "All is flux," said Heraclitus. Nothing can really be stabilized for long. To imagine that we can freeze reality in any pose is one of the elusive pots of gold that humanity is forever seeking at the end of its rainbow dreams. It is only within ourselves that we can develop lasting stability, by finding that deep, divine center around which all our human thoughts and feelings revolve.

It is the steadfastness of Taurus that all of us should seek to develop — the ability to keep plowing forward no matter what the odds are against us. This might be called a positive application of doubt, for it means using our awareness of difficulties to help us to determine how much energy we need to summon up in order to overcome them. Without such an awareness, one might plunge gaily into an empty swimming pool, or invade a powerful nation with only ten soldiers.

The famous Taurean rage may be due in part to a sense of frustration in one's efforts to keep a firm grip on things. In fact, however, such rage is a rarity. The Hindus to whom I have mentioned the ferocity of bulls in the West have expressed surprise. Perhaps our Western bulls are dangerous only because we fear them. Perhaps this is the key to the occasional rages of Taureans. It may be that when a Taurean feels himself feared or doubted by others — especially in a society where personal authority counts for so much — the addition of their doubts to his own brings him to such a level of bewilderment that, as if to restore his own sanity, he strikes out in anger. Usually, however, Taureans do their best to keep a firm grip on their own tempers, as on everything else. When they do become angry, what escapes into outward expression is generally only an overflow from a cauldron of inner frustration. Most Taureans, like the bull in the Orient, will endure much to maintain a state of peace.

The famous Taurean stubbornness also is due to fear of losing one's grip. But it has another, and more justifiable, source as well:

Like the soil in springtime, the Taurean knows that he must let the seeds of new ideas germinate undisturbed. He may harbor a plan patiently, unseen and unsuspected by others, for years. In this way also he resembles his symbol, the bull — ruminating his plans slowly and carefully. Taurus knows that you cannot force the growth of a plant. Anyone who tries to push him faster than the pace he believes necessary for him to develop an idea will find him unyielding. Yet in this he is not unreasonable; he is only deliberate.

Accompanying his deliberation are his sudden-seeming decisions and actions: the final appearance of green shoots out of the ground after spring rains. When a Taurean's plans have germinated and sprouted as long as he things they need to, and even at the very moment when the awaited opportunity presents itself at last, he may leap into sudden and vigorous action, leaving his friends gaping with astonishment.

One of the greatest lessons you need to learn, if you are a Taurean, is faith. Your own special delusion — that you must grip your realities as if your very survival depended on it — must be transmuted into determined adherence to the highest realities. Above all, as you grow in faith, learn to surrender to the Supreme Beneficence. Remember that to cling or to try too hard in anything is a sign of doubt. Learn to rely more on a Cosmic Plan in which everything, ultimately, works out for the best.

Your tendency to get a firm hold on things can be ennobled, once you learn to understand it as an energy flow *from* your inner being, rather than *to* anything specific, outwardly. Learn the principle of Karma Yoga: "action without desire for the fruits of action." Seek to get a firm hold on your own inner flow of energy. Determination and perseverance — the *way* you take hold, in other words, rather than the things you take hold of — are your personal keys to salvation from all human bondage.

To free yourself of outer attachments, learn rather to surrender than to control.

Even in giving, do not confuse love with indulgence, nor practicality with selfish greed. Learn to love *selflessly*. Learn also to dedicate your great energies to the welfare of others. In giving, learn not to impose; do not seek to possess others by the sheer exuberance of your love or friendship for them.

Complete self-surrender is a difficult thing for Taureans to learn. Yet if you can train your mind to get a firm grip on *faith,* an attitude of acceptance of life will develop quite naturally, until you discover that you need cling to nothing, for everything is yours already in God.

In meditation (which you should practice daily if you want to grow spiritually), trace all your desires and attachments back to the Venus-related heart center, or *chakra,* in your spine (opposite the heart). Become aware of the fine rays of energy that shoot out from that center to each of the multifarious things to which you consciously or subconsciously cling. With great persistence and determination, redirect these rays of energy upward toward the brain; there, draw them to a focus at the point between the eyebrows, offering them to the Divine with the affirmation: "I want only You. Receive me!" Spiritual freedom can be attained only through *nishtha* (steadfastness) in self-effort. By this technique you can go far toward raising yourself from bondage, but remember also that freedom is not something anyone can *control.* Once your rays of desire are focused in trust and love at the point between the eyebrows, offer them freely to the Lord; submit yourself to Him to be guided entirely as *He* wills.

Yogis teach that the energy in the body can be more easily directed upward if one will insulate it against the downward pull of subtle currents in the earth by sitting on an animal fur (a woolen blanket will do). Better still, they say, is to cover this blanket with a silk cloth.

To develop true Taurean steadfastness in your spiritual practices, make it a point if possible to meditate at the same hours everyday. Habit will take over, and you will begin to look forward eagerly to those hours as your time for God.

Finally, since it is your nature to hang onto reality so fervently, make that reality Truth itself. Be firmly committed to the truth — to whatever *is*, rather than to what you would like it to be. Above all, make your reality God.

> "Remember, so long as you are making the effort God will never let you down."
>
> —*Paramhansa Yogananda*

4

GEMINI

May 21 - June 20

The Sign

Gemini, ruled by the planet Mercury, is essentially a mental sign. Like Aries and Taurus, it also is a spring sign; it carries a mood of youth and exuberant enthusiasm. But Gemini's enthusiasm is felt not so much over the solid work involved in starting a project (the pioneering energy of Aries), nor over carrying through on it (the sustaining energy of Taurus), as it is over the sheer idea of the thing — whether in the thought of getting it going, or in the fascinating problems involved in carrying it out.

Gemini is the first of the air signs. As such, it suggests the first surge of gases springing up out of the earth, impatient to escape, perhaps, after long confinement underground, more intent on quick upward movement than on any particular destination.

Gemini is the sign of the twins. It often inclines one to be of two minds about things, and therefore a great worrier. If there is sufficient mental detachment, however, this same influence facilitates great mental subtlety, enabling one to see issues from many sides — a prerequisite to genuine wisdom.

The key to Gemini's influence is a preoccupation more with one's *ideas about things* than with the things themselves.

The Sun in Gemini

If your sun is in Gemini, you give supreme allegiance to the power of ideas. You seek to impress your authority on others by your mental quickness and subtlety. Unless you can learn to practice a certain mental detachment, you will incline more easily to wit than to wisdom, to cleverness than to understanding. To Geminis, the attractiveness of an idea is often its own justification. ("It's such a beautiful theory, it *has* to be true!") It is more important for you than for most people to practice non-attachment to your own ideas.

Usually clever, well informed, and good at externalizing or formalizing your ideas, you may forget (as many Geminis do) that thought without feeling will often appear to others as so much froth without substance. Intent on scintillating, you may not be sufficiently sensitive to the fact that what most people really want is not so much to find *you* charming as to be understood and appreciated themselves for what *they* are. It must have been a Gemini who invented the saying, popular in Italy: "It is better to lose a friend than to pass up an opportunity to tell a joke"!

The Gemini inclination to spin theories "in the air" can, if positively directed, lead to creative genius of a high order. If negatively directed, the theories will remain in the air; a person so inclined would rather talk than act.

There is in all of us something of this air "element." It is that capacity of the mind to break free of the limitations of habit and tradition, of physical bondage (the earth "element" in us), and soar to new heights of intellectual discovery. Creative ideas, useful inventions, new solutions to old problems — all owe their discovery to this upward-soaring, confinement-shunning spirit in man. But like the natural gases escaping from the earth, this spirit must be directed and controlled if it is to serve a significant purpose. Gemini, the last of the spring signs, must incorporate on its own mental level the basic characteristics of the other two spring signs. The Gemini must have the starting energy of Aries, lest his ideas remain only theories, and he must have the carry-through of Taurus, lest he hop restlessly from one plan to another, accomplishing nothing.

The air "element" in man tends to deny the reality of the other, lower "elements." It sees earth as a confinement: the world's coarse realities that clip the soaring wings of thought, confining its lofty aspirations to a barnyard of prosaic possibilities. Even to mix air with fire, or thought with useful energy, seems idealistically a compromise. Beautiful abstractions, one feels, should not have to serve any gross, useful purpose. Yet ideas that are not tied firmly to reality, nor objectified by practical application, have a way of drifting off into space and never being seen again. The spirit of the other spring signs — earth and fire, Taurus and Aries — is the filter through which Gemini can achieve lasting fulfillment. For inspiration to become genius, the essential ingredient is control.

The duality of Gemini is a natural correlative of his airy nature. Air cools as it rises, warms as it descends. Geminis, similarly, blow hot and cold so long as they allow themselves to be ruled too much by their minds. Their thought processes need to be channeled into consistent life patterns. Work and responsibility have a way of disciplining the mercurial mind, and are important to Geminis as a solid anchor to the bobbing balloon of their moods.

Fickleness and unreliability are characteristics also of those Geminis who are too attached to their own subjective thought processes. Just as the test of objective reality seems cumbersome and unnecessary to them in their own soaring inspirations, so also does the convenience of other people — if it doesn't happen to coincide with their own.

But if a Gemini can practice mental detachment from his own ideas and concepts about life and reality, his two-sided nature develops, rather, positive traits of versatility, adaptability, and great subtlety of thought. The developed Gemini has an ability to see many sides of a subject, and many possibilities in situations that may appear to be dead ends to other people.

If Geminis do not lose their upward-soaring zest in their struggle to come down to earth and be practical, they can develop idealism of the highest kind, an idealism which is clear-headed and realistic, but which quickly and easily rises above the spiritual doubts that often plague more plodding, literal minds. The Gemini native, more easily than most people, can achieve that faith which St. Paul called "the proof of things unseen."

If you are a Gemini, remember that your upward flight to perfection, like charity, begins at home — in a sound relationship to the realities that you find right around you. Do not become so enamored of your own opinions that you can listen appreciatively to no one else's. If, like most Geminis, you are an inveterate conversationalist, try not to become (as the saying goes) "intoxicated with the exuberance of your own verbosity." Develop mental equanimity. Too much thinking begets worry, which is the surest way of blocking out right solutions.

Mental equanimity means more than a simple refusal to become excited. If that were all it entailed, it would attract but few Geminis, most of whom view mental excitement as an essential part of the joy of living. But man's truest insights come to him, not by his *creation,* but by *perception.* Man can *reflect* truths; he cannot manufacture them. It is in order to reflect truth *clearly* that equanimity is necessary.

The teachings of yoga liken the human mind to a lake. So long as there are waves rising and falling on the surface of the water, the moon above will not be clearly reflected there. Whatever shimmering lines of light may be seen moving on the surface will seem but creations of the dancing waves; anyone so thinking would assume, erroneously, that the higher the waves, the more brilliant and perfect those lights. Similarly, anyone identified with the restless mind may think that only by increasing its waves of reaction can great inspirations be achieved. But just as the moon is reflected clearly only when the lake is calm, so also truth can be perceived truly only when the restless thoughts have been put to rest.

"Yoga is the neutralization of the waves of restless consciousness and feeling." This definition by the ancient sage, Patanjali, should be the motto of every truth-seeking Gemini. If, instead of trying to think your way through to every solution, you will hold the windows of your mind open in silent meditation, you may be amazed to see what clear answers can come to you. Especially hold open that mental window which is situated at the point between the eyebrows. Yogis teach that there lies the channel for our highest inspirations. (That is why great saints have been observed looking upward in prayer or meditation — so often, indeed, as generally to be depicted in that posture.)

The rising and falling mind, so especially the plague of many Geminis, but also symptomatic of the "gemini" in all of us, is closely related to certain upward and downward movements of energy in the spine. These two simple movements, taking place in what are known as the *Ida* and *Pingala* nerve channels on the left and the right sides of the spine, can be brought under control far more easily than can our multifarious restless thoughts. By a deliberate effort to direct these currents upward and downward in the spine,* and by bringing the mind into a sympathetic upward and downward flow with these currents, the yoga practitioner learns indirectly to control the surge of his thoughts. Thus bringing his mind under control, it is an easy next step for him to quiet it (and the spinal currents as well), and thereby to enter the stillness of true divine communion.

Mental equanimity will carry you far toward wisdom, but for *true* wisdom one needs also love. In your love for people, do not so conceptualize your feelings as to blind others, too, by your own definitions of what love is. Love is far more than your own or anyone else's definitions of it. Allow others, therefore, to express their love for you in their own ways.

Above all, develop devotion to the Supreme Reality. With a calm mind, and a heart that is completely open in its love, there is nothing in this world or the next that you cannot achieve.

> "Your mind must be kept in a state of reason, for without reason true devotion does not come. But there must not be too much reasoning because you cannot understand every-

*This technique, known as Kriya Yoga, is described in *Autobiography of a Yogi*, by Paramhansa Yogananda, and may be learned in its necessary details by correspondence from the organization which he founded: Self-Realization Fellowship, 3880 San Rafael Avenue, Los Angeles, California 90065, and from Ananda World Brotherhood Village, 14618 Tyler Foote Road, Nevada City, California 95959.

thing until you reach the ultimate state. We must have the consciousness of God in our lives. Look at the flowers and every little thing with critical insight: How could the flower evolve unless there were intelligence there? And this body — this city of cells we are carrying around: Who made that? That is how reason brings true devotion."

— *Paramhansa Yogananda*

5

Cancer

June 21 - July 22

The Sign

Cancer is the first of the summer signs. The youthful mood of spring gives way now to greater seriousness, to a growing awareness of one's own destined role in the great drama of life.

Cancer is also the first of the water signs. As such, it suggests rather the whirling eddies in a brook than the smoothly flowing river.

Cancer's symbol is the crab, which is to be found in brooks in some parts of the world, as well as in coastal waters. The grasping claws of a crab are symbolically related to the centralizing currents of a whirlpool. Both symbols suggest Cancer's focalizing power. Its acquisitiveness (when manifested on a purely egoic level), and also the extraordinary tenacity of its hold on things, are implied in the grasping claws. Its power to draw things to a focus is suggested by the centripetal flow of a whirlpool.

Cancer is ruled by the moon, the "planet" that determines what *personal* meaning things will have for us. Cancer, in the mundane horoscope, occupies the fourth house of home. The key to Cancer's influence is the wish to draw things to a *deeply personal focus.*

The Sun in Cancer

If your sun is in Cancer, you tend to view authority in terms of personal ownership. You will tend to say, "So-and-so is *my* teacher, *my* father," rather than, "I am so-and-so's student, or child." The authority that you seek to express is of a deeply personal sort. Negatively manifested, it can lead to extreme possessiveness and so be its own undoing. (The people you might seek to own would react, sooner or later, by flying away. The things you might seek to possess forever will sooner or later be broken or lost.) Positively manifested, this same trait can become an unwavering loyalty, like that of a mother for her children. Once anyone becomes a Cancerian's friend, he enters a personal universe, a "home" in which he will never be a stranger again.

There is a difference between Cancer's tenacity and the firm grip on reality that is the mark of Taurus. Taurus likes to "set" things in his environment, but not necessarily to own them. The natural impulse of Taureans is more to put things right than to put them into their own pockets. Cancer, by contrast, is at heart a home-owner. A water sign, he is more instinctively aware than Taurus of the natural flow of things. He has no delusions about controlling the flowing currents in the mainstream of life; he knows that such control is beyond his own (and probably anyone else's) power. His interests are too personal and centralized to permit him to enter freely into the mainstream. Therefore he tends, like the whirling eddies in a brook, to draw what he wants into his own orbit, and to let the rest of the current flow past him — almost as if it didn't exist. The Cancer native may even be timid in his dealings with the world, but he more than makes up for this external inadequacy by his greater-than-usual tenacity on the home front.

Directed downward from the brain, Cancer's energy tends toward withdrawal and exclusiveness, an "us four and no more" attitude that, by its excessive self-protectiveness, negates growth. If, however, one's motive in drawing things to a personal focus is not *self*-protection, but rather a wish to offer a safe haven to *all* who need protection from the roaring currents of life, Cancer's influence becomes that of a mother, drawing others like children homeward to be healed and comforted. Directed soulward, Cancer's vision expands, ultimately to see the whole universe as home: "Center everywhere, circumference nowhere."

Cancer's way to enlightenment may run dry if he tries to decentralize, or impersonalize, his view of life. Such a view will seem to him bereft of any real interest. Rather, his growth will come most easily from gradually drawing *all* things into his psychic whirlpool of self-identity, from seeing: "The whole universe is mine." As he develops a sense of universal ownership, he becomes released from the need to clutch anything to himself and call it specifically his own.

There is something of Cancer's influence in all of us. When we think in terms of "me and mine," we are acting under this influence. When we take things too personally, we are succumbing to the more negative of Cancer's qualities within us. To be aware of how Cancer affects its own natives — for good as well as for self-interest — will help us to understand how we might make the best use of similar traits in ourselves. Selfishness, for example, can be turned into a divine quality once we discover the deep, personal satisfaction that comes in making *others* happy. Personal attachment to people can be purified into a sympathetic concern for *their* highest welfare. Excessive attachment to things can be overcome by seeking to bring happiness to *others* by the purchase of those things. By observing the way these influences work on Cancer natives — who, generally speaking, manifest them most purely — we can see clearly how to handle them in our own lives. The more our whirlpool of personal interest is devoted to focusing everything in ourselves, the narrower will be not only our vision, but also our happiness. The more this whirlpool is devoted to drawing all men, all creatures, even all things into an orbit of deep, personal sympathy, the more our own understanding and happiness will expand.

But of course, it will be possible for people in whom more impersonal traits predominate to overcome also in other ways this human tendency to personalize. Such people may prefer, for example, to change the thought "me and mine," into "Thee and Thine" — thereby offering all their works to God. Some people may prefer to gaze calmly at the ego until it simply vanishes, much as a wall seems to vanish when one stares at it fixedly for some time. Many are the paths to Truth. Perhaps the greatest appeal in descriptions of the differences among the sun signs is that they point out the most common paths which different people can follow.

Though Cancer is like a whirlpool, gathering its own from the swiftly passing mainstream of life surrounding it, it yet possesses a natural relationship to the stream that would be less evident among a collection of diverse objects on dry land. The currents of a brook may flow and eddy in countless patterns, yet they are all, clearly, movements of the same thing: water. Thus it is that Cancer natives perceive a natural identity with the rest of life, even though they do not always care to explore that identity. Their need to grow spiritually by *expanding* their deeply personal vision, rather than seeing it as something to be overcome, is due not so much to any lack in their natures as to their own very special talent for universal sympathy — a talent which makes them, perhaps, the most intuitive of all the natives of the zodiac. This intuitive faculty is heightened by their receptive, rather than aggressive, natures.

If you are a Cancer native, you can also draw your psychic whirlpool to an ever-finer center within yourself, by meditation, until you come to rest in the silent soul within. This is no egoic withdrawal, no mentally diseased self-involvement; rather, it brings one to such inner stillness that the whirlpool no longer turns, the brook no longer flows, and everything — including your own little self — is discovered to be but an emanation of love from the heart of the Infinite Creator.

In Indian art, the state of enlightenment is sometimes depicted by the figure of a new moon in the forehead. The moon's influence in us, signifying as it does the personal value, or meaning, we place on things, is usually centered in the seat of ego at the medulla oblongata, at the base of the brain. The positive pole of this center is said to be situated at the point between the eyebrows. When our inner "moon" of personal involvement becomes centered completely in this positive pole — in other words, when the center of our being shifts from the lower brain centers to the highest in the frontal lobe — we achieve divine enlightenment. One good practice, then, for you "moon children" (so called because the moon rules Cancer) would be to concentrate at the point between the eyebrows, and to associate all your sense of personal meaning in life with that point — the Divine center in man — rather than with the petty ego.

The definition given by the ancient Hindu sage, Patanjali, to the state of divine enlightenment is: *Yogas chitta vritti nirodh* — yoga (divine union) is the neutralization of the waves (literally, whirlpools) of feeling" (Yoga Sutra 1:2). *Chitta* signifies, in a general sense, the lower mind. The disturbances in the lower mind that obstruct divine union are, as Paramhansa Yogananda explained them, the tumultuous feelings, the attachments, the likes and dislikes, of the heart. Their movements, or *vritti,* are usually explained as waves, but literally mean whirlpools, or eddies: a fitting metaphor for — guess whom! You Cancerians should take this definition deeply (and literally) to heart, by striving always to overcome your egoistic likes and dislikes. The magnetism you exert should be that of divine, all-healing love, not of possessive attachment. In your focalizing power you should seek always to serve as instruments of the Divine.

If you hope to attain enlightenment, it would be well for you to meditate regularly. Helpful for everyone, but perhaps especially for you, would be a room, or at least a screened-off portion of your bedroom, set aside especially for meditation. Places develop subtle vibrations, depending on the sorts of consciousness with which people permeate them. If you fill your meditation room (or screened-off corner) with meditative peace, it will help you to go deep every time you sit for divine communion.

Try sitting very still and straight when you meditate. Face east if possible (your intuitive awareness should make you more sensitive than most people to the harmonious magnetic rays that flow from that direction; north, too, is a recommended direction), and drop your mind down to what is sometimes called the "cave" of the heart.* Rest peacefully here. Feel this cave to be your true home, your true

*This psychic heart center, or *Anahat Chakra,* is located in the spine opposite the physical heart. Remember that the spine passes more or less through the center of the body. What you feel along your back are only superficial protrusions.

temple. Imagine that the harmonious radiations from the east are emanating from an altar placed toward the east in your own heart-temple.

Now see these radiations becoming rays of the purest light — flooding your heart, transforming the darkness of selfish desires into brilliant shafts of divine love.

Now spread these rays outward — filling your body, your home, the whole universe. *You* are that Infinite Light!

You are that Infinite Love!

> "Above everything else, be loyal to God. Give more time to Him, and not to the little duties of life which will be gone one day. For therein lies the greatest delusion, when we think that our duties are more important than our love for God."
>
> —*Paramhansa Yogananda*

6

Leo

July 23 - August 22

The Sign

Leo is the sun's own house. It is the second of three summer signs, and the second also of three fire signs. Its placement at the center of both these triplicities reflects the sun's position in the solar system, and suggests the essential consciousness that is imparted by this sign.

The second of the summer signs, Leo comes at that time of the year when most forms of vegetation have achieved their full maturity. Leo's influence, similarly, represents man's sense of authority at its height. It is as if Cancer's need to establish a personal focus had been realized, making possible now a sense of confident self-expansion.

An interesting corollary may be seen in the way

stars are believed to have been formed. The condensation of the nebulous clouds of gases that become a galaxy is thought to be accompanied by countless smaller eddies within the larger mass. These eddies are more substantial than the surrounding gases. Perhaps it is by their rotation that they draw more gases into their orbit — after the fashion of whirling eddies in a brook. At any rate, at some time the increasing amount of matter becomes sufficient to condense into a huge ball; the intense pressures that are created in the process result in the formation of a fiery star.*

The key to Leo's influence is similar to that of its ruler, our own star, the sun: a strong sense of personal worth, of *personal authority*.

The Sun in Leo

If your sun is in Leo, you seek to exert your authority over others by being, simply, yourself. Your natural desire, in fact your expectation, is to exert your authority by shining, not by coercing others. You assume that others will be impressed by your

*Very ancient tradition speaks of the "elements" as consisting of ether, air, fire, water, and earth (in that order). If we think of *ether* as representing the primordial energy out of which the first atoms are born, of *air* as representing the nebulous gases, *fire* the stars, *water* the molten state of matter as it cools still further, and *earth* as matter that has cooled sufficiently to become solid, we find that those "elements," seemingly the fruit of ancient ignorance, very clearly epitomize the *elemental stages* of creation. Astrology does not assign this same sequence to the "elements," but evidently this science was developed at least in part within that ancient tradition.

views. If anyone is not, you may become distant and withdrawn, in attitude like a star, reminding yourself that you cannot expect people to enter your orbit who aren't close enough to you to really know you. This tendency to affirm people's distance from you by becoming distant yourself is a fault, for it only brings you unnecessary pain, enforcing an isolation that you don't really want. (After all — you think — aren't you, too, a sort of human star on a rank with all the others of the base human galaxy?) Fortunately for you, however, most people *do* find you impressive.

The influence of Leo tends toward noble, or at least calmly impressive, actions. As the sun is the center of the solar system, so Leo tends to be the center of his world — not in an absorbing way, like Cancer, but in an outwardly radiating, life-giving manner. Leo natives, like those of Aries, are often leaders of men, but in their leadership they have the self-possessed majesty of a king; their authority is central, unchallenged, and secure. Theirs is not the quick, restless energy of Aries leaders.

If the inner energy-flow of a Leo is not in proper balance, he may explode outward like a star-nova, consuming life instead of nurturing it. Such an imbalance of energy produces egotism, and an inclination to prefer gaudy show to real substance, outward glamour to real merit — a tendency, in short, to concentrate more on the *effect* of one's outward radiance than on the true source of it in oneself. Such Leos, by forgetting to stoke the fires of inner worth, become depleted at last, and rather inconsequential people after all.

Yet it is important to all Leos, and not a sign of egotism, for them to know that there are others who receive, and appreciate, their light. To be totally bereft of this feeling is, for a Leo, to be bereft of his own deep sense of mission. Such a Leo becomes lost: self-pitying, suspicious of others, resentful of every imagined slight, rejecting a world that, he believes, has rejected him. He is like what remains of a star after its explosion as a super-nova. (Astronomers say that, in all likelihood, there are *no* remains. Similarly, in such people, there is nothing left of their true Leonine qualities.)

If a Leo's inner flow of energy is harmonious and calm, he will manifest that natural magnanimity of complete self-possession in which the thought of self can be forgotten, not in a spirit of self-effacement (never that!), but because there is no inner feeling of need to protect the ego. He is king, and expects matter-of-factly to be recognized everywhere as such.

Leos have a natural sense of personal authority. It is only human, however, in any matter that is really important to us, to seek the safety of extra support. Since authority is so vital to a Leo, he may try to bolster his own sense of it by claiming some even higher authority (whether human or divine) for everything he says and does. Used insensitively, this tendency can make him ruthless and dictatorial — the unfeeling bureaucrat, or the proud instigator of religious persecutions — or, on a more day-to-day level, simply the sort of person who tries to win people to his own point of view by presenting it on the authority of someone else. Used sensitively, however, the sense of ruling (or shining) as an instrument of some higher power can give one a gracious mien, a kindly, generous, and noble spirit, a natural dignity that instinctively draws others up to his level instead of impressing them with the relative insignificance of their own positions.

Leo's focus is on giving, not on receiving. On a higher level, this can mean a warm, generous spirit. On a lower level, it can imply a tendency to walk serenely but rough-shod over others, with a remarkable lack of concern for their feelings.

We all have something of Leo in us. It is reflected in our need to achieve a sense of personal worth. At times all of us go begging for approval or sympathy from others. Then, whether from rejection or from a sudden sense of our dignity, the Leo in us asserts itself, and we say, "How foolish of people to think that *I* need *them*! I am complete in myself. If others need anything from me, let them come to me!" And then it is that we face in ourselves the essential struggle of every Leo: whether to emphasize our own worth by setting ourselves above (or apart from) others, or to emphasize it by generously sharing with them the inner strength that we now feel. The one path leads toward barrenness and emotional isolation; the other, toward increasing inner radiance and a sense of genuine personal fulfillment. Unfortunately, human capacity for self-deception being what it is, some people get bogged down in a middle ground between these alternatives. In trying to give others their "strength," they only succeed in boring them to tears. (Many Leos, alas, are classic bores!) The way past this mire lies in developing a genuine interest in other people. To be *only* a Leo would be a misfortune. We need to develop other inner qualities, also. Specifically in this case, we need to develop two most un-Leonine traits: the ability really to *listen*, and *receive*.

If you are a Leo, your progress lies in a genuine self-offering in the service of others. You need above all to realize your inner affinity with the sun, your ruler, whose gifts to the solar system are its rays of light and energy. Your giving, too, should be expressed less in the form of things or of specific deeds than by a kind of sympathetic and strength-giving, psychic radiation.

In your search for Truth, you must allow your own sense of authority to make you all the more appreciative of authority itself, as an eternal principle. Open yourself in calm understanding to the rays of wisdom and grace flowing into your soul, in meditation, from the Supreme Sun, the Spirit.

And then — still in meditation — radiate your love and blessings outward to all mankind.

> "When the rose is crushed by the hand or stepped upon by the foot it gives off a sweet fragrance. So must your life be. Give only kindness and love to those who do evil against you."
>
> — *Paramhansa Yogananda*

7

VIRGO

August 23 - September 22

The Sign

The summer signs, as I have said, represent a growing awareness of one's destined role in life. Of these three signs, Virgo is the last. After Leo, it might seem that further growth of this particular kind of awareness would be impossible. But there are different kinds of development, any one of which, taken alone, leads to a dead end. No human fulfillment is absolute; therefore no human fulfillment is permanent. Leo's strong sense of personal worth, of radiating in strength and blessing upon his fellow creatures, finds its further human development not in shining even more strongly, but in turning back upon itself with an age-old question: "Why all this involvement? What is it all for? Are there no higher realities to be sought?" The sun, too, returns through Virgo to its starting point, the equinox. Virgo in the sun's annual cycle marks the first point of real questioning of life's basic values.

Virgo is ruled, as Gemini is, by the planet Mercury. It is, then, a mental sign. But it is also an earth sign, indicating that its mental influence is heavier than that of airy Gemini. Instead of charm and wit, Virgo inclines toward critical questioning.

The earthy quality of Virgo, the second of the earth signs, is different from that of Taurus. In Taurus the soil is soft and rich with sprouting expectation. Now it is late in the summer; the ground has become parched and dry. Separating cracks appear in the earth's surface, and clods of dirt no longer fuse moistly together as in springtime, but stand distinct and separate from one another, easily to be crumbled into smaller particles. This is the mood of Virgo: a season for examining things in fine detail, for probing for distinctions between things, for separation and analysis.

Virgo means *virgin,* symbol of a pure mind encased in a physical body. Virgo's clear faculty of discrimination also is, in a sense, physically encased, for it is directed toward questions of immediate and practical value, rather than toward airy theoretical abstraction.

The key to Virgo's influence is the ego's dawning realization of its need to develop *discrimination.*

The Sun in Virgo

If your sun is in Virgo, you seek to impress your

authority on others by your powers of discrimination. Discrimination (the ability to tell right from wrong, truth from error) may translate itself in your mind merely as logical analysis, with no question of values attached. Analysis in turn may translate itself as attention to detail which may still further become infatuation with details, or even outright fussiness. And so it is that Virgos can run the gamut from men and women of great and magnetic wisdom to colorless clerks whose sole purpose in life seems to be to see that one set of inconsequential details is in every minute respect consistent with another set of inconsequential details. The vague imprint of the least developed Virgos may still be seen in the highest types — like the faint scars of an ancient wound. The highest potentials of this sign slumber fitfully in even the least evolved of its natives. It is almost as if the most routinized, rule-conscious, procedure-bound, narrowly structured, nit-picking Virgo to be found in the lowest echelons of a government office recognized somehow that he had a much higher calling, and buried himself still further in his mound of petty details out of abject fear of the labors implied. (The same might be said, of course — each time with emphasis on a different human trait — of every sign in the zodiac.)

Virgos have a natural gift for any work involving attention to fine detail. Where the natives of some of the other signs seek fulfillment in expanding their energies, Virgos seek it in concentrating them. Where an Aries will try to blast his way through an obstruction, a Taurean to push his way through it, and a Gemini to jump over it, a Virgo will search carefully for a hole just big enough to squeeze through.

Virgos have a natural love for putting things neatly and carefully where they belong. They like rules, procedures, and the patterned, orderly existence these imply. Even when not especially conventional in their behavior, Virgos are usually fairly conventional at heart; keenly conscious of the struggle involved in breaking out of their sense of social forms, they may put on a show of being "naughty boys," but, like children running away from home, they rarely get past the front gate. (They know that if they did go much further, they'd be lost. A sense of structure is something they must have, to survive.)

Every human quality contains its own built-in system of pluses and minuses. Virgo finds challenge in fine detail, but it is possible, after all, to wedge oneself into such a small nook that one can no longer breathe. Exhaustive research is not needed to prove that Virgos need breath as much as the most hearty and hallooing of us. They also need freedom as much as any of us. They may seek their freedom by learning to function efficiently within some existing structure, or by trying (usually without success) to break out of all existing structures, but they will never truly find the freedom they seek until they develop to its fullest their discriminative faculty, which is present in all Virgos — at the very least in their fascination for fine details. Discrimination is their special technique for breaking out of the traces that bind mankind. It is also one of the finest tools that the human race as a whole has been given for its salvation, for the real bondage of man consists of the heavy, self-tied ropes of his own delusions. Virgo's special fulfillment lies in using his fine gift for analysis to untie those complicated knots. His intelligence was not given him merely to solve the Sunday crossword puzzle.

The way to fulfillment is always forked with many by-paths. One temptation for the Virgo is to devote his powers of analysis to analyzing *others*. He may sincerely mean to be helpful; at least, he will tell himself that he does. For Virgo is a season of harvest; the attitude of Virgo natives, similarly, is one of genuine, and often humble, service, of analysis with a *useful* purpose, and never merely to prove abstractly how clever they are.

The weakness of the human ego being what it is, however, what they mean to do and what they actually accomplish are not always identical. Even honest criticism, unless it is sincerely invited, and then tendered with a feeling of genuine sympathy, may open wounds without effecting a cure. Unfortunately, when the critical faculty is at work in the operating room, sympathy is usually left to wait outside in the corridor. Feeling and reason work harmoniously together only when there is true ego detachment from both qualities. Virgos, despite their wish to be helpful in the advice they give, have a reputation for being hypercritical. They tell themselves they are only being helpful, when in fact they are only exasperated any time someone disturbs what they consider the neat and proper arrangement of the universe.

Virgo's highly developed critical faculties, giving him as they do a natural flair for fine details, make him in consequence a perfectionist. It is important to his growth to train himself to relate every detail to a broader picture of life and reality. Otherwise he may so isolate himself in his very *special* specializations that he cuts himself off from life itself, becoming only a sort of intellectual shell, or a mechanical drudge. There is a definite tendency among Virgos on all levels not to see the forest for the trees. A spirit of egoic non-involvement in their work and in the details of daily living helps them to develop the calmness necessary to see past the preoccupations of the moment to the deeper issues at stake. Concentration *with deep calmness* is an important key to every Virgo's development.

The key for Virgos, in fact, if they want to grow psychologically and spiritually, and not simply to plow themselves ever deeper into a rut of routine, is to remember their symbol, the virgin. The concept of a pure mind encased in a physical body suggests their own need to function realistically here in this work-a-day world (which they very easily manage to do), and yet to achieve also that sort of mental detachment which is the mark of a developed discrimination.

If you are a Virgo, you need, for your spiritual growth, to turn your critical gaze away from others and backward upon yourself. It is easier for you than for most people to see through the delusions to which the main run of humanity cling. Strive, therefore, to use this talent to banish all delusions from your own consciousness. Penetrate to deeper and deeper levels of true insight, until you achieve at last the calm dispassion of a sage.

Your mission in life is not *at any level* to spend your time pointing out to people the absurdity of *their* delusions. On every level, rather, it is to show them by your example the freedom that can be developed by exercising true discrimination: the freedom that comes from doing one's duty in life without personal attachment. Through your example of this spirit, others, too, may learn to work conscientiously *in* the world, and yet inwardly not be *of* the world. Such spiritual freedom is the only freedom that any man will ever find.

There is a practice that you may find helpful. It is summed up in the Sanskrit words, *neti, neti,* — "not this, not that." That is to say, whatever comes into your mind, look behind it — refer it — to the greater reality of which it is an expression. A friendly face? Realize that what really attracts you is not only the person it represents, but the broader principle, Friendship, of which your friend is a manifestation. A wish to possess something? But will you ever find anything, *anywhere,* that you can truly own? That which truly *is* your own you cannot possibly lose. That which is external to yourself cannot but be lost. You cannot, therefore, ever really own anything external. This very ego that seeks to own things is but a crumbling clod on a dry field; it is not your true self. *Neti, neti.* The deeper you seek, the further you will trace everything back to but a single Cause: the One, Eternal Spirit.

Virgos aren't the only virgo spirits around! We all have some of this Virgo-like capacity for discrimination. If we misdirect it into outward criticism, or into an excessive concern over petty details in our lives or in our work, we, too, may become hypercritical of others, nagging, judging, or merely overly fussy. But in every human failing we find only one side of a coin, of which the other side is a human virtue. Remember the saying, "Judge no one but yourself." If we will direct this same critical gaze inward upon ourselves, we will find it invaluable for our inner growth, especially if in our self-judgment there is no self-condemnation, but only a detached effort to understand and to improve.

The path of discrimination alone may seem dry; it is certainly not for everyone. But without *some* capacity to discriminate, no one can progress very far in life.

Finally, if you are a Virgo, try sitting very still every day in meditation, and trace your own sense of "I" back to its source. Who is it that is thinking? Who is it that is questioning this "I"? Your thoughts are not really *you*. Your very questioning is not you. Alfred Lord Tennyson, the great poet, used as a boy to achieve a state of ecstasy by the simple repetition of his own name. Inadvertently, perhaps, he had stumbled on a great secret. Practice this technique yourself. Try stepping behind the veil of your own ego. What you find there, so countless sages have claimed, will be your own Infinite Self!

> "True discrimination does not come through a process of logical reasoning, but as a revelation from within. It is born of calm meditation and divine contact."
>
> —*Paramhansa Yogananda*

8

LIBRA

September 23 - October 23

The Sign

At 0° Libra, on about September 23rd of each year, the sun re-crosses the equator and moves into the Southern Hemisphere. For the next six months the countries north of the equator will experience longer nights than days. These might, then, be called astrologically (as well as literally) the "dark" months. Yet darkness implies many things that these months are not. In India's great Scripture, the Bhagavad Gita, one reads: "That which is night to the worldly person is day to the yogi" (II:69). The inner world seems dark to the worldly person only because his mind is not calm enough to perceive the inner light. The same Scripture passage states also: "That which is day to the worldly person is night to the yogi." The inner light, once it is clearly perceived, is so blazing as to make common daylight appear as darkness by comparison. The last six months of the year are allied to the soul's inner search for the One, Perfect Light.

The first three of these months belong to the season of autumn. The ego's search for its outward role in life, as reflected in the summer months, gives way now to what might be called a search for inward identity. And spring, the season of new leaves and a corresponding mood of life affirmations, finds its complement in autumn, its opposite season, when leaves fall, and when the ego, like nature itself, withdraws — not in death or in world rejection, but in private affirmation of its own inner reality.

Aries is the first of the spring signs; Libra, the first sign of autumn. The fiery starting enthusiasm of Aries is offset in Libra. Where Aries says, "First let me get this project going, and then I'll know where I stand," Libra says, "First let me know where I stand, and then I'll know how to start on that project." Where the first instinct of Aries is to become involved, that of Libra is to withdraw from over-involvement.

Libra's is an autumn mood. It harmonizes well with the bright colors of fading leaves. A keen sense of beauty is intrinsic to Libra's influence, for Venus rules this sign as it does also Taurus. But autumn's beauty soon blows off into the sky on strong gusts of October wind. Autumn's is an affirmation not of *living* beauty so much as of an eternal principle. What remains — the dead, fallen leaves — fertilizes the soil. To Libra, beautiful things are more inwardly than outwardly nourishing; they feed an inner sense of harmony that is seen as the real meaning and purpose of all beauty.

Libra is the second of the air signs. Its influence suggests air spreading outward in search of equilibrium. Highly volatile, like air, Libra's influence indicates no definite, calculated search, but rather a free-flowing, windy-one-day, calm-the-next spirit very much like the changeable weather of autumn. Libra represents the ego in its first, tentative search for inner identity.

The symbol for this sign is a pair of scales, suggesting a need to achieve in all things a state of balance and harmony. Ruled as it is by Venus, Libra's balance is on a feeling, rather than on an intellectual, level.

The key to Libra's influence is the ego's search for *inner harmony*.

The Sun in Libra

If your sun is in Libra, you seek to express your authority by externalizing your inner sense of harmony. This sense is so much your authority in life that, if you can possibly help it, you will never act in any matter until you feel inwardly *right* about it. Your typical response to any proposal is, "You'd better let me think about it."

Your love of harmony expresses itself objectively in your human relationships. True friendship and true love mean much to you. Your unselfishness, especially where close friends are concerned, may give the impression that your interest is focused wholly in their interests, not in your own. Alas, human egoism is no such fragile eggshell that mere birth in a particular sign can demolish it. That you are so often unselfish in your human relationships is due to the fact that outward harmony serves as an affirmation of your own need for *inner* harmony. If any conflict arises, however, between this inner need and those of your friends, you will give no more of yourself to them than would the next person, and may even seem the more callous because of the sudden change in your attitude. It must, in fact, be added that you are at all times *less* likely than many people to want really to enter into the lives of others. Because you desire harmony at almost any price, you will tend deliberately to blind yourself to the anxieties, frustrations, and disappointments of others, preferring to soar through life at an altitude where even towering waves seem no larger than ripples.

The tendency of the air "element" in human nature, is, as we have seen in Gemini, to rise high above coarse, earthy realities. In Libra, because of the rulership of Venus, this soaring takes the form of lofty idealism rather than of abstract ideas. Where Gemini's mood is one of restless upward movement, the air "element" of Libra seeks a steady, high altitude. But the need in both cases is the same. Unless this air element in man can be related to solid, practical realities, its tendency will be to become so rarefied as to lose all touch with our planet and its crude, but actual, demands. Libra can inspire an "ivory tower" consciousness. It needs the balance of those more earthy qualities which Venus achieves in its other sign, Taurus.

Those who are developed enough in themselves to receive Libra's influence on all levels of their lives will seek to harmonize the highest with lower realities. The perfect modern exemplar of this principle was the great master, Lahiri Mahasaya, whose life Paramhansa Yogananda described in his *Autobiography of a Yogi.* Lahiri Mahasaya, himself a Libran (born September 30th), emphasized in his life and teachings the ideal of the "yogi householder": one who fulfills his obligations to family and community, and who yet finds time to devote to spiritual pursuits.

Librans, usually, are born peacemakers and unifiers. This essential influence of their sign may, however, become blurred if the lens of ego has not yet been finely enough ground, permitting only a selfish focus on *personal* harmony. Libra's natural gift for finding a common meeting ground between issues will then result in mere opportunism, and a tendency to "play both ends against the middle." The old Hindu writings state that Libra's rays create an attraction to alchemy. This expresses the Libran's skill at changing left to right, and up to down, in his search for a midpoint of balance. It is a talent that must be used wisely, or the end result will be inner confusion, not peace.

Even if the lens of ego is well-ground enough to permit a depth of focus, the polishing must continue until there is no sense that one is looking through a lens at all. Otherwise the harmonious rays of this sign will continue in subtle ways to be distorted, and the native will not achieve that perfect harmony which he desires. For man was meant to serve as a channel for higher vibrations than his own. Even to think, "I do this" or, "I do that" is to interfere with the flow of those high forces. Egoistic activity affects people differently, according to their own natures. In Librans it produces over-anxiety, of which perpetual vacillation and irresoluteness are very often the companions. Those Librans in whom activity is not paralyzed by anxiety will often, out of very fear of imbalance, flee so impetuously from one extreme that they end up at the other. It is as if, finding the scales too heavily weighted on one side, they tried to correct the imbalance by frantically snatching all the weights from that side and simply dumping them onto the other. But a swinging motion, once started, is not easily stopped. Thus it is that many Librans, despite their ardent desire for inner harmony, actually become the most unstable natives of the zodiac.

The rays of Libra, more so than those of most signs, are exceedingly delicate, and must be received with great sensitivity if life's dual scales are to be brought to a state of lasting balance.

This is a point that should be heeded by everyone, Libran or not, who hopes to find harmony in his own life. For Libra's rays reach all of us in varying degrees (depending on our own openness to them). If we remember that harmony is something not so much to be created as *received*, through our attunement with higher realities, we shall be able to find it no matter what our sun sign. Sensitive Librans may have a head start on some of us, but no one, certainly, has any monopoly on divine states of consciousness.

Balanced moderation in all things is a universal ideal. People who veer constantly from one extreme to another find overall progress very slow. Even-mindedness is their fastest route to perfection. To be overwhelmed by misfortune, or to give up hope when once — or even again and again — we fail or fall into error, is to identify ourselves with imperfection; it is to deny strength to our true nature as eternal souls. We should not even be overjoyed at good fortune, nor take too much pride in success, for worldly fulfillment of every kind is so fragile that at any moment a quick stumble on life's path might shatter it into pieces. Our happiness must be identified with inner soul-consciousness if it is to endure. The Libran instinct to withdraw from involvement is a necessary part of the search for harmony. We all need to draw back a little bit from things, to accept both success and failure even-mindedly, identifying ourselves inwardly with neither.

Librans, and indeed anyone who seeks lasting inner harmony, should endeavor always to seek out the underlying unity in life's apparent diversity. This is to be a peacemaker in the highest sense: ever to see the One Spirit resting at the heart of all dualities. "He who watches Me everywhere, Him do I watch. He never loses sight of Me, nor do I lose sight of Him" (Bhagavad Gita VI:30).

A good meditation for Librans, especially, would be to concentrate on the horizon line of the ocean, or on any fine line dividing one thing from another, and try to penetrate into the hidden realms suggested by that line. "God," Paramhansa Yogananda said, "forever rests on the horizon line between all opposites." A straight line is one-dimensional. By penetrating that single dimension one's consciousness passes through into the dimensionless world of the Spirit.

The superconsciousness rests, similarly, on the horizon line between consciousness and subconsciousness, between wakefulness and sleep. Every night, try slipping into superconsciousness just at the borderline of slumber.

The seat of superconsciousness in the body is the point between the eyebrows. Ego-consciousness, that great distorter of inner harmony, is centered in the medulla oblongata at the base of the brain. (It is from here that the united sperm and ovum first begin the creation of the human body.) Instead of allowing your watchful awareness to originate from this ego center, feel it to be centered at the point between the eyebrows. Gaze upward with half-open eyes, and concentrate on the horizon line that divides the darkness above from the light below. If you concentrate deeply enough, you will plunge through that line into the ever-peaceful, ever-harmonious realm of ecstasy which is the natural state of the soul.

Libra natives, by increasing relaxation and trust in the Divine Power to set everything right, by acting firmly with a consciousness of peace instead of trying to wrest peace from a hostile world, can grow in time to become perfect instruments of God's peace.

"There is a fine line where the sky touches the

ocean. That is what God is like. He is subtly settled between good and evil, light and darkness, sickness and health, and all other dualities. That is why I love to watch the sky kissing the water. It reminds me of His hidden presence."

— *Paramhansa Yogananda*

9

Scorpio

October 24 - November 21

The Sign

Scorpio is the second both of the autumn and of the water signs. This doubly central position suggests, as it does with Leo, an ego that is centered firmly in itself. But there is a difference. The fact that Scorpio is an autumn, not a summer, sign suggests self-assurance more in terms of inner identity than of outer, worldly position. And Scorpio's designation as a water sign suggests determined movement, usually toward some definite goal, and usually with a minimum of concern over any devastation that might be wrought along the way. (Leo, by contrast, is willing simply to shine its calm strength upon the world.)

Scorpio, throughout much of the Northern

Hemisphere, is the month when the last leaves fall off the trees, and when the frost and cold begin to make themselves really felt. Windows are closed, cheerful fires are lit in the fireplaces, and people congratulate themselves that they have warm, comfortable homes to retreat to. Scorpio's mood is one of self-affirmation — not necessarily in an egotistical way; often, rather, in determined pursuit of its own goals. The winds of opposition may howl, and the air of outward opinion may chill, but Scorpio rests determinedly in himself, and seems almost to derive added, if grim, comfort from the fact that the weather outside is so unfavorable.

Scorpio's expression of the water "element" differs from Cancer's. Instead of the inward-drawing eddies of a mountain brook, Scorpio is like a strong, silently flowing river, moving with quiet purpose through life's varied scenery, self-enclosed between high embankments, uninvolved in whatever lies outside its own path — and (remembering rivers in flood) perhaps better kept so!

Scorpio is the opposite, and therefore complementary, sign to Taurus. Where Taurus expresses its sustaining energy outwardly, and feels a need to prove itself on the testing ground of the world, Scorpio's power is essentially inward, more or less indifferent to any directions and values but its own.

According to ancient tradition, Mars, the planet of energy, is the ruler of Scorpio, as it is also of Aries. But here its energy is controlled and focused, like a laser. Because Scorpio falls in the eighth House of death and hidden realities, and because its influence also is deep and subtle, more modern Western astrologers assign its rulership to the recently discovered planet, Pluto. At least one authority, however, insists that Pluto belongs properly to Aries, because both represent regeneration, which is inseparable from death, or from the end of an old cycle. And yet, the outer planets in our solar system are believed to be related more to eternal than to immediate, mundane affairs. In this respect, certainly, Scorpio — the river winding ever in search of the Infinite Sea — is better suited than Aries to be Pluto's home. In any case, both of these planets have a special bearing on this sign: the focused energy of Mars, and the power to seek deep within oneself for revitalizing strength, which is believed to be the result of Pluto's influence.

The symbol of Scorpio is the scorpion. Though usually to be found hiding under rocks and in dark places, the scorpion is by no means a timid creature. It rushes out to attack anyone presumptuous enough to disturb it. Its venom is powerful, though seldom deadly. Wherever on this earth it is to be found, the scorpion, though rarely showing itself except reluctantly, is a power to be reckoned with.

The key to Scorpio's influence, whether directed creatively or destructively, is *hidden power*.

The Sun in Scorpio

If your sun is in Scorpio, your sense of authority springs from mystical depths. Even when you are, as you may be, a strict traditionalist, winding your way like a river through well-established channels, your traditionalism will carry the weight almost of a mystic cult. You may tell yourself that you derive your authority from others, or from society in general, but in reality it springs from deep within yourself. If you attribute it to others, you will do so not from any special humility, but rather because your instinct is to hide from others your true source of power.

In fact you are self-sufficient, a self-starter like your Martian brother, Aries, but in a deeper, more deliberate manner. You can be surprisingly indifferent to the feelings of others, and can sting suddenly with your words, like the scorpion — not necessarily out of malice, but probably from a tendency to think, like the scorpion, that the best defense is a quick offense. Though sometimes sharp with words, your real wish is to be left to your own pursuits; your sting therefore is seldom intended to destroy. In fact, where friends are concerned, you tend to be intense in your loyalties, as in everything else.

You incline generally to an intensity that, if not controlled, may border on rashness. If your sense of inner power is not harnessed, you may leap into things with both eyes closed, never considering the possible danger, never counting the cost.

By ill-considered action, the Scorpio's outbursts of energy may destroy even when they were intended to create. This is the peculiar dualism of the creative energy, over which Scorpio is said to rule. It is a power that may be directed towards the destruction of self as well as of others. (Witness the scorpion's legendary practice of stinging itself to death if it sees no escape from danger.) But if this energy is kept sensibly under control, its power for constructive action is enormous.

Because your power, if you are a Scorpio, comes from deep within yourself, you rarely tip your hand before you act. You understand, better than any other sign, the truth that talking about a project may dilute the power to act on it. Your instinct for secretiveness differs subtly from that of your zodiacal counterpart, Taurus.

Taureans, too, like to nurture their idea-plants underground, safe from the prods and challenges of other minds, but this tendency in them marks a lack of self-assurance, a wish to be certain before they act outwardly. The Scorpio is not likely to be plagued by such fine misgivings. Where the Taurean's real interest lies in the time when the plant will bloom at last in beauty for others to enjoy, the Scorpio may be content to keep even the plant's matured beauty to himself. Scorpio's realization that power is best channeled when it is focused, not diffused, gives him a subtlety of thought that is rarely encountered to such a degree in other signs. Misused, this subtlety can take the form of outright deception — of oneself as well as of others.

There is, or should be, something of Scorpio's influence manifested in all of us. We need always to act from a strong inner center, that our actions may carry weight, and not be only like the passing froth on an ocean billow. We need to learn first to conserve, and then to channel, our energies, and not to scatter them through publicizing them too much to the world, not to exhaust them by over-exuberance or rashness. Paramhansa Yogananda once said to a new, and exceptionally eager, disciple: "Don't be like a straw fire in your enthusiasm. Dynamite, if it is exploded in the air, accomplishes no great good; it may even be destructive. But if the time is taken to bury it carefully underground, it may be used to create useful tunnels. So is it with enthusiasm. It must be brought under control; only then can it serve a useful purpose." This factor of control suggests something of Scorpio's influence (or lack of it) in our lives. Because every sign contains its own opposite, many Scorpios, not sufficiently responsive to this aspect of their sign's influence, substitute intensity for control, and plunge with the greatest fervor into self-indulgence, and a way of life from which control is virtually absent.

If you are a Scorpio, you may need to learn to equate these two: intensity and control. You will never find true fulfillment, moreover, but will wind pointlessly through life and never really "find yourself," until you discover that the true goal of your life's journey is no temporal satisfaction, but the infinite sea of divine awareness.

Be not like a river in flood, devastating the land of other's feelings, but respect their rights and privileges. They have their course to follow. You should stick to yours.

It is a part of the power of cosmic delusion for man to be constantly tempted to direct his energies outward, away from himself. To do so purely and selflessly, as a conscious channel of divine grace, is good; it is not a temptation. But the labyrinth of egoism is a complex one indeed, and man is inclined by the very power of his delusion to squander his spiritual earnings almost as soon as he gains them.

Scorpios must learn to turn their sense of control backwards upon themselves, to develop *self*-discipline. Their temptation may be, as they develop the dispassion that is born of self-control, to feel that they must trample as freely over the feelings of other people as they have learned to do over their own. As self-discipline grows, there does come a certain divine ruthlessness — a joy in demolishing one's own encrusted ignorance of ages. Take care, once this quality develops in you, not to waste it outwardly again by directing it toward others — *especially not if you find the slightest pleasure in doing so*. For though it will seem to you that you would not be treating them any differently from the way you treat yourself, there *is* a difference. You are, in a sense, *asking* for that kind of "pleasure"; they are not.

Normally speaking, the destructive urge in you is one of the negative directions that your strong creative energy can take. If, however, you turn this destructive power toward the demolition of your own ego, it can result, paradoxically, in what may be your supreme creative act, for it will give shining inner birth to soul consciousness.

A saint once said, "Live in this world as if only you and God lived here." If you will share your deepest thoughts and feelings with God, talking to Him in the second person as if He were always waiting for you to turn to Him, asking Him constantly to guide your thoughts and actions, your self-directedness will be expanded and ennobled.

In addition to that, you will find great release from the confining pressures of egoism if you devote your great energies to the service of others. A life lived for self alone, on the other hand, will bring you at last to a kind of living death.

Yoga teaches that the spine is like a river, its currents of energy flowing constantly, though most people are seldom aware of them. The principal task of yoga practice is to strengthen these currents, and at the same time to increase one's sensitive awareness of them. The true "river of baptism," extolled in many religions by the outward symbolic act of bathing, is the spine. Danda swamis, a class of monks in India, carry straight staffs to remind themselves of their need to live more in the spine, and to keep it always erect that the currents of life may flow through it freely.

"Make straight the way of the Lord," said St. John the Baptist. Sit very straight and still in meditation. Feel the river of life in the spine,* and direct its flow very slowly and deliberately upward to the brain, and thence to the point between the eyebrows. At that point feel that your river of energy and light is entering at last into the great ocean of cosmic light.

If the Scorpio nature is to advance spiritually, it must be through stern self-discipline. The advanced Scorpio will be a true *vairagyi,* or ascetic, focusing all his energy on the task of achieving self-mastery.

> "Always remember that seclusion is the price of greatness. In this tremendously busy life,

*The technique of Kriya Yoga, mentioned already in this book, would help you greatly to become aware of this inner river of energy.

unless you are more by yourself you can never succeed. *Never, never, never.* Walk in silence; go quietly; develop spiritually. We should not allow noise and sensory activities to ruin the antennae of our attention, because we are listening for the footsteps of God to come into our temples."

— *Paramhansa Yogananda*

10

SAGITTARIUS

November 22 - December 21

The Sign

Sagittarius is the last of the autumn signs. Autumn's search for inner identity, which reached a peak of seriousness in Scorpio, relaxes now into happy self-acceptance. The festive (and, for anyone who is spiritually sensitive, the divinely joyous) mood of this month is due to more than the fact that Christmas is approaching; it is actually the mood of Sagittarius. Those who are born under this sign experience something of its mood the year around.

Sagittarius is the last also of the fire signs. It represents the upward-soaring tips of flame in a bonfire, flickering and vanishing into the night. Where Aries (the first of the fire signs) represents starting energy, and Leo (the second fire sign) represents the full blaze of a work well under way, or of an ego that has found its own place in the world, Sagittarius represents the ideal outcome of all striving — the release of energy for broader application, and of thought for more universal understanding.

Sagittarius is commonly represented by a centaur (half man, half horse) shooting an arrow up toward the stars. This appears to be a Greek enlargement on a more ancient symbol: the archer (*Dhanu,* as he is still called in India). But the meaning remains the same: the upward evolution of the soul from the animal to the human state (or, for man, from animal preoccupations to the self-possession befitting his dignity as a human being), and its aspiration to evolve still further: from ego-consciousness to cosmic consciousness (symbolized by the stars). The horse is an ancient symbol of power; here it signifies that the archer's aim for the stars is no empty gesture.

Sagittarius is ruled by Jupiter, the planet of expansion. Expansion of consciousness is the very essence of spiritual development. Most Western writers, evidently unaware of this truth, relate Jupiter only to ego expansion: the acquisition of wealth, power, and earthly happiness. This is a very much lower expression of Jupiter's influence. In the ancient tradition, Jupiter is the planet above all of spiritual development. In Hindu astrology the name for this planet is *Guru.* A true guru is far more than a teacher. He is one, rather, who by the subtle influence of his free consciousness lifts his receptive disciples out of the bondage of delusion. ("As many as received him, to them gave he power to become the sons of God" — John 1:12.) Similar, though more general, is the power of Jupiter. Through its subtly expansive influence the consciousness of man is helped gradually* to evolve to the highest possible state. The human "centaur" becomes an enlightened sage.

A key expression that is often used for Sagittarius is *upward aspiration*. But a more all-encompassing expression would be the soul's unending *search for universal awareness*.

The Sun in Sagittarius

If your sun is in Sagittarius, you seek to impress your authority on the world by universalizing whatever presents itself to you for serious consideration. Your mind soars quickly (sometimes too quickly!) from particulars to universals. In your work you see the broad view; petty details probably bore you. In your friendships, unless you can find someone whose mental influence gives you the sense of expansion that you need, you tend more to be a friend to all than to develop one or two close relationships. In love, you are more likely to be a good pal than an ardent Romeo or Juliet. (As one writer has aptly put it, you tend to let your spouse carry the emotional load.) Whatever your present understanding of things, your instinct is to expand it. This you may do by relating it to ever broader realities. Most Sagit-

*The Hindu Scriptures speak of spiritual progress as occurring in twelve-year cycles, the time it takes Jupiter to make one complete revolution of the zodiac, and to transit all of the houses in an individual's horoscope.

tarians, however (since few men are wise), will try to satisfy their expansive instinct by insisting that everyone in the world be bound by their own personal vision of reality.

Your reaction to Jupiter's expansive influence will depend on your own sensitivity. Essentially, Jupiter's role (and that of Sagittarius, its own sign) is to help man to expand his awareness toward cosmic consciousness. So strong, however, in many people is the grip of ego that Jupiter's influence may give them merely the "inspiration" to impose their own values on everyone they meet. Other Sagittarian's — overeager, perhaps to embrace infinity? — overlook, and often stumble over, little pebbles that lie right under their feet. (Prosaic details are the proverbial nemesis). It is up to you Sagittarians individually to make your mental lens so clear of egoism, and of the restlessness and confusion which ego inspires in you, that the rays of Jupiter and Sagittarius reach you in their purest form.

Because release from confinement is accompanied by a sense of joy, Sagittarius, with its power to lift the mind into the freedom of universal vision, is a joyful sign. Sagittarians usually have a remarkable capacity for enthusiasm. Indeed, they tend to see everything through the filter of their enthusiasm — a capacity which can invest the very Devil himself with a halo of perfection: or, if the native is hurt or disappointed, can attribute the blackest of sins to the most shining angel.

The influence of Sagittarius is dynamic, not static. Sagittarians proverbially enjoy plenty of movement and change in their lives. If one can pace himself to a moving bus, he will be able to leap onto it without difficulty. If he misguages the speed, however, he may be thrown to the ground. The outward-moving, joyful influence of Sagittarius, similarly, can free anyone from delusion who moves with it sensitively. Anyone who cannot attune himself truly to these vibrations, however, will be cast down by the very power that might have carried him to the heights. This is to say that expansion of consciousness must entail a growing awareness of the vast world beyond the little circle of one's ego; it cannot come by imposing one's personal interests on the universe. Paradoxically, perhaps, the mood necessary for true soul-expansion is *receptivity* — a difficult word, alas, for many Sagittarians to comprehend. The archer's arrow of aspiration can reach the stars only if it is not tied down by the heavy cord of self-interest.

One whose assignment in life is to "shoot for the stars" may, if he is worldly, feel that such a target is too hopelessly vague. In this case, he may content himself with shooting for its own sake, regardless of whether he hits anything or of whether there is anything really to hit. Like an office employee who, not fully comprehending a job he has been given, makes a brave show of activity by shuffling papers frantically right, left, and everywhere, many a Sagittarian becomes so intoxicated with his own exuberance that it matters little to him that he has no idea where he is headed. He shoots his arrow of energy indiscriminately, and ends up with an empty quiver. It is only when one learns to focus all his energy into a single ray of aspiration that his enthusiasm can become a clear channel for, and also a pathway to, divine joy.

Probably the most important thing you need to learn, if you are a Sagittarian, is to take the trouble to make a really good arrow. Details may bore you, but without careful — even painstaking — preparation the flight itself may be a failure. Don't, by your impatience to embrace all of life, join those multitudes of Sagittarians who cling to nothing longer than a few moments, thinking by a large number of shallow experiences to attain that universality which is found only in deep calmness, and in total self-forgetfulness. For the truth is that man cannot fly by his own power. He must exercise the patience necessary to make himself a perfect instrument for the Divine.

Once you have learned not to intrude the vibrations of your ego into your enthusiasm, and once you have developed *true* impartiality (not the superficial "everyone's friend" attitude of one who coasts through life with a perpetual grin), you will be able to achieve that expanded awareness which is the essence of wisdom.

It would be well for all of us, no matter what our sun signs, to bear in mind these positive and negative characteristics of Sagittarius. They apply to all of us in varying degrees.

The instinctive goal of all life is expansion of awareness. The obstacles to this expansion are for everyone basically the same: first, man's attachment to his little ego; second, a tendency for him to seek to overcome his littleness, not by giving up the ego in favor of a larger, divine, identity, but only by expanding its sphere of influence (more money, more power, etc.). A third obstacle, more specifically Sagittarian, is the tendency to "think high thoughts" while overlooking the need for daily, practical application of spiritual principles.

It is a mark of greatness to see all things in relation to universal realities. Sagittarians do this more naturally, perhaps, than many people, provided they are not distracted by egoic involvements. Their fondness for the broad view of every subject is something which all of us should strive to develop, lest an endless concern over prosaic details paralyze our creative efforts. Indeed, even our faults and weaknesses are, in a sense, but minor details, born of our consciousness of egoic limitation. A broader view of reality can help us to overcome them finally and forever. In this we see the strength, as well as the weakness, of Sagittarius, for while inattentiveness to details is often the reason for failure, a truly universal view attunes one to the all-powerful soul, before whose divine effulgence no failure is possible.

If you are a Sagittarian, your progress lies above all in seeking *by soul-consciousness* to universalize your awareness. Meditate regularly. View the world increasingly through the eyes of your inner peace. See the Lord, whom you contact in the inner silence, as residing equally on "altars" everywhere, smiling at you from every flower, from every tree and cloud. Develop what Paramhansa Yogananda called, "other-mindedness" — the faculty for seeing God behind all His earthly disguises.

You, as a native of a fire sign (Aries and Leo natives — and anyone else who wishes to do so —

might also practice this technique), would find it helpful to meditate on fire. Think of it not as hot or painful, but as a cool, liberating energy. Offer into it your impurities, your worries, your pride. Visualize this divine fire spreading its joyous flames consuming every idol that you have carved mentally for the worship of your own ego — your pride of possession, of family, of reputation. Transmute all of these into the fragrant, upward-soaring smoke of divine aspiration.

You might even build an actual fire. Cast bits of wood into it with deep attention to what you are doing. Feel that every stick represents some fault; offer it mentally into divine flames. In this way, too, you can be purified.

Jupiter's outward influence as the "guru" of our solar system aids in the slow process of spiritual development. This process can be vastly accelerated once one learns and applies the science of *inner* astrology — the secret of harmonizing the inner man with universal, cosmic influences. This is the science of Kriya Yoga, mentioned already in these pages. The Hindu Scriptures state that, by outward astrological influence alone, man would require at least a million years to achieve cosmic consciousness. By Kriya Yoga, great yogis have said, it is possible to achieve this state in one lifetime.

The Hindu name for Jupiter (*Guru*) suggests an important spiritual truth. If Kriya Yoga is practiced with a sense of inner attunement to one's own guru, it speedily lifts one to enlightenment. For as *Guru* (Jupiter) represents the saving rays of Divinity in the objective world, so the grace of the human guru, directed consciously and specifically to the God-thirsty disciple, represents the rays of salvation in the inner, subjective world.

Remember, when you meditate, that it is not enough to imagine that divine joy will come to you someday, probably, provided you stick grimly to your chore of daily practice. Meditate *with* joy if you want to find joy. Sit no longer than you can do so with enjoyment. (It may take a few months of practice, however, actually to reach this state of enjoyment.) The true path to God is not a boring, but a joyously soaring, one.

Feel joy, either in your heart or at the point between the eyebrows, and visualize its rays spreading outward like a divine fire, consuming all human sorrows and delusions, transforming the entire universe into the ever-blissful light of Infinity.

> "Happiness comes, not by aimlessly thinking about it, but by *living* it in all the moods and actions of life."
>
> — *Paramhansa Yogananda*

11

CAPRICORN

December 22 - January 19

The Sign

Capricorn is the first of the winter signs. Winter is a time of outward stillness. The leaves have fallen from the trees. The sap has ceased to flow. Snow covers much of the land, hushing men's footsteps, and burying the endlessly varied bushes, trees, and shrubs under an impartial quilt of white. In this season Nature abandons for a time her outward frivolities. Even in warmer climes the air seems charged with an awareness that life is more than gay flowers and laughing brooks, that what truly matters are eternal principles. Winter symbolizes that period in the soul's growth when the ego, its autumn months of self-questioning finished, seeks fulfillment in relating to broader realities.

The winter solstice marks the point at which the

sun's influence on man's consciousness is most "inward." The loss of ego-consciousness which this solstice implies marks the culmination of Sagittarius's expansive influence. For Capricorn, it implies only the beginning of a serious search for impersonal realities.

Capricorn, the last of the earth signs, represents earth in its last stages of refinement: the rocks, minerals, and gems into which it condenses over eons of time.

Capricorn is ruled by Saturn, the planet of contraction, of concentration. Saturn's rulership here suggests great powers of concentration, and an ability to condense amorphous facts into small precious stones of truth.

Capricorn is traditionally represented by a strange creature: half goat, half fish. In India, the goat part of this mythological monster is replaced by an antelope. One thing these two animals have in common is sure-footedness, indicating Capricorn's keen sense of earthly reality. Matter, however, is only a manifestation of deeper, spiritual realities. If one's sense of reality is keen enough, he will be able to pierce this veil of matter, and to perceive the omnipresent Spirit underlying all natural manifestations. Spirit's formlessness and vastness are often described metaphorically as an ocean. The realism of Capricorn, in other words, when it is developed to perfection, leads to the state of divine self-mastery, a state wherein one finds himself at home equally on the firm "soil" of this world and in the great "ocean" of Spirit.

Another quality that many types of antelopes

share with the goats is an attraction to high mountain peaks. Capricorn's influence, similarly, calls people to scale the peaks of consciousness — to see below them the panorama of reality in all its vastness — if they would fulfill their destiny of balanced outer and inner, temporal and eternal, wisdom.

The key to Capricorn's influence is its power to awaken in the ego *a desire to bring reality into sharp, impersonal focus*. A secondary key word for this sign is *concentration*.

The Sun in Capricorn

If your sun is in Capricorn, you tend to want to impress your authority on others through the medium of your keen sense of reality. This sense can range from shallow cynicism to the deepest wisdom, depending on your own level of spiritual maturity. Essentially, if your inner, concentrative energy is directed primarily downward, it will make you a down-to-earth, practical materialist who may feel little sympathy for esthetic or spiritual ideals. An upward direction of this same energy, on the other hand, can lead to the heights of divine wisdom. The more you can direct these rays of energy upward in aspiration, rather than downward in a spirit of life negation, the clearer your vision will be. In any case, your deepest instinct is always to see behind the facade of things, to penetrate to the heart of whatever reality you are sensitive enough to comprehend.

The goat (your symbol) is a serious animal, with great powers of endurance. Authority (your sunsign) is, for you, something to be taken seriously.

You receive it seriously; you exert it seriously. Because of your earnestness, your powers of endurance can be phenomenal. It is not necessarily that you are somber by nature. In fact, in your relaxed moments you probably have a charming (though often unsuspected) sense of humor. Your vivid sense of reality gives you a keen appreciation of the unreal, the ridiculous, a vision which may express itself in a quiet, wry wit, or even (in more extroverted Capricorns) in a real gift for burlesque. Your powers of concentration, however, make you impatient with froth when you are trying to seize the essence of a matter.

If the main direction of your inner energy is downward, your powers of concentration can make you an opportunist of the worst kind, blind to all normal scruples, which you will see as a mere fog obscuring your pragmatic goals. Capricorns of this low type may, because of an inborn gift for organizing, make excellent gangsters, or ruthless politicians who shield their cynical actions under a label of "realism."

If your energy is less blindly, but not yet spiritually, directed, you will see the essence of reality in more normal human values. You will be scrupulously honest, straightforward, and just. You will, in fact, direct your powers of concentration toward an intense affirmation of these values, measuring your very worth in terms of your ability to deal with any practical, worldly situation that may arise.

The more your inner energy and concentration are directed upward, the more clearly you see the shallowness of most human interests. In this case, you will focus your sights on progressively deeper levels of reality, until, ultimately, your single-minded goal becomes the realization of Eternal Truth. At this highest level, Capricorn, so often considered the most materialistic of the twelve signs, becomes in a sense the most spiritual. For it is not materialism that marks Capricorn natives, but a power of concentration, and single-minded concentration of all of one's powers is the prime condition for spiritual advancement. ("Thou shalt love the Lord thy God with all thy heart, and with all thy soul, and with all thy mind, and with all they strength: this is the first commandment" — Mark 12:30.)

Another negative trend is observable in this sign, apart from a possible descent into outright materialism. Implicit in every human trait is, as I have said elsewhere, its exact opposite. We have seen how a realistic outlook can, if misdirected, become a mere rationalization for the most deluded manifestations of self-interest. The power of concentration, similarly, constitutes for the Capricorn a sort of vocation, which he is at liberty to accept or reject. Like a genius who wastes his mental powers on drunkenness, Capricorn natives (perhaps with a thought of, "Not yet!") are sometimes known to recoil from the inner call to focus their energies. In this case, their powers become dulled; their lives, inconsequential.

Another negative trait that you may need to watch, if you are a Capricorn, is a tendency to become over-suspicious of others — a misdirection, merely, of your capacity for realism.

Capricorn's influence, like that of every other

sign, is activated in certain directions by the planets that are posited in it, or in aspect to it, at the time of birth. Its *general* influence, however, is constant on every human life. Our own inner natures, moreover, are a composite of qualities which the stars and planets merely help us to energize, but which would exist as surely were there no external influences to affect them.

It would be well for all of us to develop some of Capricorn's qualities: its capacity, for instance, for unsentimental realism. Life is not always (indeed, very seldom) quite as it appears to be; its hard realities trip us up constantly. Keats's equation of truth with beauty is valid only if we accept that that which is not also true cannot be truly beautiful. A lovely face may conceal a venomous heart. A beautifully phrased poem may express ignoble sentiments. An opportunity, seemingly heaven sent, may only have been thrown out of heaven to get rid of it. We need to learn to deal with life as it is, not as we may wish that it were. It is only thus that we may awaken at last from the universal dream of cosmic delusion.

Paramhansa Yogananda, himself a Capricorn, stressed in his teachings the importance of another quality, one which, in the last analysis, is only epitomized by this sign. "Concentration," he said, "is the key to success." He taught techniques of yoga that can help everyone to develop this essential faculty. (These techniques may be learned by correspondence course from Self-Realization Fellowship, the organization which he founded in Los Angeles, California, and from Ananda World Bortherhood

Village, 14618 Tyler Foote Road, Nevada City, California 95959.)

If you are a Capricorn, or if you want to develop Capricornian virtues, try acquiring more of a questioning than a judgmental attitude. So long as the spirit of realism in man sees itself only in a perpetual crusade against self-deluding sentimentality, its vision will remain fixed, and narrow. Realism has its own growing to do. We grow when our critical gaze is focused, not on others, but on ourselves. Capricorns who feed on judgmental attitudes become set in their ways, suspicious of others, and unreceptive to truth. Their very realism, because it closes certain doors to reality even while opening others, becomes but a guardian for their ignorance. Pit your sense of realism, therefore, against itself. Ask yourself always, "But *am* I being realistic?" You will find that often that which seems the least substantial is, in the deepest sense, the most true.

The earth "element" in man, expressed especially in the earth signs (Taurus, Virgo, and Capricorn) suggests certain human qualities that are important for everyone to develop: firm resolution, unswerving dedication to one's ideals, immovability on questions of truth, honor, or justice. Meditation on the different "elements" can help us to develop their allied virtues.

Sometimes, therefore, in your meditations, try visualizing your body as a rock, so firm that you can't move it, so heavy that no one else could move it. Sit perfectly still with a straight spine. After a few minutes you will lose the desire to fidget. Then visualize your mind, too, as a rock, so immovably fixed that no thought, no emotion can sway it.

The seat of concentration in the body is located at a point midway between the two eyebrows. (That is why, when people concentrate deeply on anything, they tend to frown slightly.) Gaze upward, and concentrate your mind with fixed attention at that spiritual point. If any thought enters your mind, offer it up to that thought of mental fixity. Any sound that you hear, or any other sensation that invades your attention, refer it mentally to the point between the eyebrows. Feel that all thoughts, all sensations have their very origin at that point.

Once the mind becomes perfectly calm and concentrated, joyous spiritual perceptions will come of themselves; you need not try to create them, and in fact you would not be able to do so if you tried.

How sensitively you respond to Capricorn's rays depends primarily on the strength with which your inner energy rises in aspiration in the spine. In all your seeking, in all your questioning, in even your most practical problems, offer yourself mentally to the Lord at the point between the eyebrows. Your deepening perceptions of reality will expand eventually to embrace the far-flung shores of cosmic consciousness.

> "When we go to a tragic motion picture and see death and suffering on the screen, we may leave saying, 'What a fine picture!' Why then can we not say as much of this motion picture of life? For the truth is, we are only shadow players on the screen of life. We are immor-

tals sent here on earth to act our roles and then depart. We should not take the play seriously. Whatever picture is showing, we should not let it disturb our minds. Let us just say, 'This is a good picture. I am learning much from this experience.' If you can face life with this attitude, you shall see the light of eternal bliss dancing through all life's experiences."

— *Paramhansa Yogananda*

12

AQUARIUS

January 20 - February 18

The Sign

Aquarius is the second of the winter signs. As we look over what we have covered of the seasons so far, a certain rhythm emerges.

The first sign of every season is called a cardinal sign; it sets the tone for that season. Spring, with its mood of youthful eagerness and expectation, is epitomized by Aries, the sign of starting energy. Summer's emphasis on the search for one's own outward role in life is captured by Cancer, with it strong personal focus on things. Autumn's mood — the ego's search for inner self-identity — is established by Libra. Winter, and the ego's desire to relate to broader, universal realities, is especially the mood of Capricorn.

The first, or cardinal, signs only set the direction for their respective seasons; theirs is a mood of searching, not of fulfillment. It is in the second, or middle — the so-called *fixed* — signs that an apex of fulfillment is reached. Thus, in Taurus the buoyant expectations of spring are no longer confined to tentative (and often abandoned) beginnings, but are seized determinedly with both hands. In Leo, the middle of the summer signs, the ego's search for its outer role results in the calm certainty that what was sought has been found. In Scorpio, the "fixed" of the autumn signs, the ego's search for inner identity culminates in a firm sense of inner completeness, of self-possession. And in Aquarius, the desire to relate to broad, universal realities passes from initial discovery to a deep sense of attunement with those realities, a recognition of their essential *rightness.*

Aquarius, according to modern astrologers, is ruled by Uranus, the planet of initiative and originality. More ancient tradition (still followed in India) considers Aquarius to be the positive sign of two that are ruled by Saturn, the planet of contraction. Saturn, in its positive aspect, signifies *dharma,* eternal law, and man's spiritual duty to grow to ever higher levels of attunement with that law. No rule can be applied in the same way to everyone, for different people have reached many different levels of spiritual unfoldment. The only specific rule that may be given is one of general direction: One's growth must spring from *within,* and must reach ever upward, ever outward toward infinity. Spiritual development, in other words, must be self-motivated. More important than any outer discipline is the seeker's inner aspiration.

Closely allied to this spirit of self-motivated aspiration are those more Uranian qualities: initiative and originality. We see, then, that Uranus also is apt as a ruler of this sign. But because its nature has not yet been explored as deeply as Saturn's has, it would be best if these planets were considered to rule Aquarius together.

Aquarius is the last of the air signs. It suggests air no longer rising to great heights as if to escape earthly contamination, but rather descending from those heights, offering vitality and cool, refreshing breezes impartially to all.

The symbol of Aquarius is the water bearer, pouring water out of a jug in blessing upon the earth. Why water, since Aquarius is an air sign? The reason is that water in ancient times symbolized life and spiritual baptism. The true gift of Aquarius is to inspire the understanding that man's highest duty is to serve as a vessel, merely, for higher truths.

The key to the influence of this sign is *a sense of the essential rightness of universal law, and a corresponding wish to bring all things into harmony with that law.*

The Sun in Aquarius

If your sun is in Aquarius, you seek to impress your authority on others by impressing upon them your own vision of universal law. From this central trait spring the many subtle ramifications of your complex personality, one that can be simultaneously sociable, yet innerly a loner; given to chronic worry, yet innerly strong in faith; dogmatic, yet innerly fair and open-minded; progressive, yet innerly closed to new ideas; humanitarian, yet innerly perhaps the most impersonal of the twelve signs.

You combine in your nature the broad vision of Sagittarius with the attentiveness to detail of Virgo. A perfect balance of these traits, liberally seasoned with that rarest of human qualities, wisdom, will place you among the greatest of mankind — as a person of deep vision, with the capacity to transform high thoughts into practical action. Such a perfect balance is, of course, not easily come by. Even when it is achieved, it can cause widespread misunderstanding among your associates and contemporaries. They will find it difficult, for example, to reconcile your apparently sincere feeling for them with your broader vision of duty, which permits you sometimes to treat them as if they were mere brush strokes on a canvas of impersonal reality. Those who look to you as their personal friend may sometimes suspect you of insincerity in your friendship for them. Those co-workers, on the other hand, who admire your devotion to duty may sometimes see in your generous nature the potential betrayal of their cause.

Few people realize as clearly as you do the necessity for compromise between a given ideal and its practical applications. Fewer people still are willing to see themselves as mere beneficiaries of that ideal — to be befriended, for instance, because you believe in friendship, rather than because you believe in *them*. Your friendly nature leads some people to feel that you are more bound to them, personally, than you really are. Your idealism causes others to expect a greater devotion to abstract principle than your actions will seem to show. As I say, a perfect balance of your inner and outer nature can crown you with greatness. But to be great, alas, is to be misunderstood. It causes people to expect much of one; in your case, they rarely get from you quite what they expect.

Duty is your true god: your sense of duty to your own abstract vision of truth, your sense of duty to bring people and things into harmony with that vision. Since wisdom is a rare gift, your field of vision may embrace very much less than the universe. Since tact is a rare virtue, your efforts to harmonize people with your own ideals may amount only to meddling in their affairs. On the highest level, Aquarius's gift of inner grace can manifest itself outwardly in the purest kinds of humanitarian love. On lower levels, it may produce only busybodies, with a "universal" view no broader than their neighborhood's need for a better garbage collecting system, and an irritating habit of talking garbage to everyone they meet.

An imbalance between inner vision and outward action can result in outright contradictions. Inwardly, one may feel oneself to be full of universal love; outwardly, he may see people only as threats to that ideal, and may suspect his truest friends of infidelity. ("I love humanity; it's people I can't stand.") Inwardly, one may be full of faith in the divine law; outwardly, his efforts to harmonize his surroundings with that law may result only in worry. If the outer task seems too hopelessly large, the very loftiness of one's ideals may paralyze all action, resulting only in laziness. And if ever an Aquarian's energies become negatively directed (perhaps because his ideals seem unattainable), he may, with a sort of negative idealism, denounce idealism itself. In this case, he will lose all sense of personal mission in life, and become (until he picks himself up again) a lost soul.

The greatest failing of Aquarians is a tendency to think that everyone in the world should be bound by truth as they themselves see it. Their inclination to objectify their own ideals can amount to an imposition on the freedom, and perhaps on the even broader vision, of others. Without a wise understanding that truth has many facets, and that even the most absolute truths may legitimately be applied in various ways in this relative world, Aquarian natives may descend to the narrowest dogmatism.

Aquarians, because of their wish to objectify their inner ideals, are often gregarious. Their focus, however, is less on the people they mix with than on the abstract sense of rightness that causes them to be sociable. Inside, Aquarians tend to feel quite alone in the world.

Because of their wish to bring people and things into line with their own values, Aquarians are often progressive, innovative and original. It would be a mistake, however, to expect them to be as open to the ideas of others as their liberal attitudes suggest. The Aquarian's motivation springs from an inner vision; he is less sensitive to outward opinions than one might think. Indeed, he will often appear unreasonable, because, while he does his best to get others to "see reason," his own understanding comes to him from unworldly realms — from mere whim, if he is undeveloped spiritually; or from divine intuition, if he is wise.

One human vice to which few Aquarians will stoop is pettiness. The rest of us might begin here to contemplate the possible influence of this sign on our own natures. For pettiness is born of the sense of ego-limitation, which is the very essence of all human delusion. A deliberately broad view of life can rescue us from suffocating confinement of self-interest. A deliberate effort to share our blessings with others, if sensitively directed and not merely imposed on them, can help us in our efforts to expand our consciousness. It would be well for everyone to remember a Sanskrit saying, truly Aquarian in spirit: *Yato dharma, tato jaya* — "Where there is *dharma*, there is victory."

If you are an Aquarian, it would be well for you always to try to see yourself in as impersonal a light as you see the rest of the world. For while abstraction comes easily to you, normal human egoism may prevent you from including the subject — you — in your view of objective reality. In this respect, there is a curious duality to your nature: You can be impartial to everyone else, yet yourself be deeply hurt by every unintended or imagined slight. You may tell others exactly how they should live their lives, yet remain so "impersonal" about it all that you never think of applying your own good advice to yourself! "Do as I say, not as I do," is a motto which you might do well to refine.

Probably you have made many attempts in your lifetime to become more personal in your friendship with others, if only because you know they expect it of you. Just as probably, your efforts have ended in failure. Just when you thought that you were getting really close to people, your strong sense of duty blurred your focus on intimacy. You may as well face it, your real key to happiness lies in becoming *truly* impersonal: in surrendering your own ego, too, into the Infinite Reality, and opening yourself to becoming a pure instrument for divine grace. In this way the Law will work through you perfectly, uplifting others even without any conscious effort on your own part.

It is necessary for you to work in some way for the welfare of others, for otherwise your inner perceptions will lose touch with reality. But the more you develop spiritually, the more you will discover that to serve truly is not to see oneself as the server.

Strive always to broaden your vision of truth. Don't stunt your spiritual growth with dogmatism.

Above all, see God acting through you. See Him in all men, in all things. Realize that, pervading the universe, there is but One Reality. Live more and more in that blissful awareness.

It would help you to practice all the principles of meditation that have been taught so far in this book.

You particularly, as an air sign, and anyone else who finds this practice attractive, might sit calmly in meditation and visualize yourself surrounded by infinite space. Gaze mentally millions of miles to the left of you; to the right; in front; behind; above;

beneath. Gaze within yourself and see there, too, an infinity of space. *Shunya* the Hindus call it: nothingness. Soar lightly in this infinite void, freer than any bird.

Then slowly, from your own inner center, expand outward in all directions to infinity a sense of universal love and joy. All beings are being bathed in your love and joy. This, and this only, is the Law, the Supreme Reality.

> "I have made my heart a wilderness, that the wild flowers of Thy love might blossom there."
>
> —*Paramhansa Yogananda*

13

PISCES

February 19 - March 20

The Sign

Pisces is the last sign of the zodiac, the last of the winter signs, the last of the water signs. Herein is the symbolism of the circle justified, for often in life it so happens that that which seems last ends up being the first: The ugly duckling turns out to be a swan; the handicapped child, driven to greater efforts by his misfortune, becomes a leader among men; the poor youth with little education is able more easily, because unencumbered by the weight of traditional thought, to ride the waves of social change to success. Failure itself, if rightly understood and accepted, can be a very special sort of victory. Life's progressions, unlike those of human thought, are never in a straight line. The old man in many ways resembles the child. Wisdom has much in common with innocence. The greatest sinner, having seen enough of evil to reject it totally, may suddenly find himself a shining star among saints. Often it is not at what point we join the search, but the earnestness with which we seek once we have joined it, that determines how soon we shall reach the goal. As Jesus said, "The last shall be first" (Matt. 20:16). (Christianity, in fact, is in many ways a truly Piscean religion.)

With Pisces, the sun covers the last stages of its annual journey, moving northward to the vernal equinox, and, in terms of the rhythm of the season, advancing toward what might be called a new lease on life. What mood accompanies this return?

If a journey has been profitable and instructive, it will end in an upward-soaring mood of happy anticipation and readiness for new things. If, on the other hand, one's travels have brought losses and sorrows, the return may be accompanied by a mood of life-negation and weariness. More than likely, since most journeys are a combination of success and disappointment, these contrasting moods will swim together in the same stream of consciousness — first one, then the other rising to the surface. Such are the conflicting moods of Pisces. The very weather of this month reflects them, with its frequent and unpredictable alternations of winter winds and spring zephyrs. To master these moods, one must recognize failure itself as but a doorway to fresh opportunity. (As Yogananda put it, "There is *no such thing* as misfortune. There is only opportunity!")

The last sign of every season is what is known as a mutable sign. The apex of power has been reached in the middle, or fixed, signs. In the mutable signs there is a drawing away from this apex — in Gemini, from heavy commitment; in Virgo, from ego-involvement; in Sagittarius, from over-intensity. At the same time, there is a mood of preparation to receive the next season's influences. In Pisces we find, similarly, a withdrawal from winter's stern focus on reality, and a reaching out to life with that kind of universal sympathy which anticipates the ardent and joyous recommitments of spring.

Pisces is said to be ruled both by Jupiter, the planet of expansion, and by Neptune, the planet of psychic sensitivity. We see in this sign the Jupiterian faculty for service, as opposed to the Saturnian (which we found expressed in Aquarius). Pisces represents not so much the call of impersonal duty as a genuine feeling for people and for all life, a wish to spread out like water and enter in at the cracks of all experience. The rulership of Neptune here, also suggests profound sensitivity. Pisces is a sign of understanding by means of deep empathy, never by cold analysis.

Pisces, the last of the water signs, suggests a river spreading out to form a broad delta before it enters the sea. It enriches the land even in the act of finally abandoning it. Such is the nature of Pisces: giving, yet free, and never so free as when it gives the most.

The symbol of this sign is two fishes, traditionally depicted swimming in opposite directions: one, toward the sea and freedom; the other, upstream to spawn, and thereby to embrace once again the cycle of earth life: rebirth, and bondage. Implied here is a choice: If the ego is willing to relinquish its hold on self, the Piscean feeling of empathy for all life can empower the soul to merge forever in the great ocean of Spirit. If the ego is not yet innerly poised and secure enough to offer itself freely into the cosmic sea, this same feeling of empathy will cause it to enter once again into limited, worldly relationships. In this case, the two fishes will have a further significance: the giving up of old ways in preparation for the assumption of new ones — a fitting symbol for the end of one astrological year and the approach of a new one.

The key to the influence of Pisces is *universal empathy*.

The Sun in Pisces

If your sun is in Pisces, you seek to exercise your authority over others through your capacity to identify with them completely. Pisces appears on the surface to be the most purely self-giving of all of the signs. So long, however, as the ego is not prepared by inner maturity to relinquish its own for a greater identity, the law of the jungle will obtain. The ego is at no loss for tricks to preserve itself. Pisceans are adepts in the fine art of control by indirection. You may find that you exercise authority over others by insinuating your way into their lives through your sensitive ability to see them through their own eyes, and to see life as they see it. You will use this gift cynically only if you yourself are cynical. Otherwise you can be quite charming, and few will mind (or even realize) how completely, by your self-identification with them, you possess them. You can win them to you by giving them something that everyone wants: understanding. In your deep empathy you can be among the most divinely magnetic of human beings. Yet your gift of empathy, like water which is your element, is a fluid thing. Friends of yours who seek to hold you to them in a firm grasp are dismayed when they find you flowing out through their fingers. They must learn that the only way truly to hold you is to receive in cups of sincere appreciation, whatever you may choose to give them, knowing that the power can only rest with you, the giver, to decide what you will give, and when, and how much. So determined are you, indeed, to let no one seize from you what you are not prepared to give freely, that at the least hint of pressure from others you may withdraw into yourself. There are subtle laws that govern right giving; no one understands them better than you do. You will take much in silent suffering, however, from those whom you love before actively resisting their impositions.

You see self-giving as your true role and destiny in life. If anyone scorns your self-offering, or tries to prevent you in the exercise of it, you will fight for it as if for very self-preservation. People seldom suspect how very adamant you can be in clinging to what you feel you *must* do in life. Your essentially feminine outlook gives you a sort of protective "mother" instinct toward your own actions and ideas — your "brain children."

Universal empathy implies a strong, mystical

sense that is not susceptible to the ploys of human logic. If anyone tries to pit his common sense against your own inner sense, his arguments might as well be the moonlight striking on your ears for all you will hear of them.

You are gifted at seeing any given subject in countless different lights, and at seeing a thousand ways of approaching it, where others might see only one. You may use this gift to try to get your own way in life, arguing your cause from every possible angle. (Pisces natives often make good lawyers!) A more sensitive direction of your talents, on the other hand, would be not to try so much to get your own way with others as to help each of them to find *his* right way in life. For you were born to heal, to serve.

Direction is the key to your own, as to everyone else's growth: the *way* in which you direct your energies. Those two fishes (your symbol) swimming in opposite directions suggest the options open to you. If you encourage your inner energies to flow upward in a spirit of life affirmation, your empathy will broaden into cosmic love. If, on the other hand, you allow them to flow downward, in a spirit of world negation and weariness, your empathy may express itself only passively, through a dreamy nature that prefers imaginary to actual experience, and that may even feed its dreams on drugs or alcohol.

For it must be understood that Pisces only gives an *inclination* to empathize. The *quality* of one's empathy will depend not on the outer sign, but on one's inner sensitivity. The same general influence that can make one person deeply responsive to the joys and woes of the world can make another, color-blinded by egoism, see woe everywhere merely because *he* is woeful, or gladness merely because *he* is glad.

In fact, there is a strong inclination here to identify yourself wholly with whatever you perceive, such that if it seems sad you will assume its sadness wholeheartedly to yourself; if glad, you will be completely glad. There is a tendency, therefore, to moodiness, and consequently toward exaggerating the significance of anything that invites your serious attention.

Your sun in this sign indicates the way in which you exert your inner sense of authority over others. The fact that yours is the last sign of the zodiac suggests your own special technique for impressing yourself on others. By voluntarily placing yourself last, you know that you improve your chances of somehow getting placed first, by others. If you are weak, you will probably use this knowledge to play on people's pity in an effort to get them to carry you. If you are strong, you are probably also mature enough to know that more can be accomplished by enlisting people's cooperation than by commanding their obedience. If you are spiritually wise as well as strong, you know that man can accomplish far more as an instrument of higher powers than by arrogant self-assertion.

I said earlier that Christianity is a piscean religion. (Its early symbol, too, was a fish.) The frequent emphasis of Jesus on placing oneself last, on turning the other cheek, on walking the extra mile, on inheriting the earth through meekness rather than by force, have tended to give an impression that Christianity is a religion for weaklings. The popular conception of the perfect Christian is a person who creeps around corners for fear of being bowled over by someone in a hurry. It is true that Jesus counseled what might be called an absorbing, rather than an aggressive, approach to life. His whole teaching — which was born after the vernal equinox had entered the constellation Pisces — breathes the spirit of this sign. It was perhaps the teaching best suited for lifting people out of their delusions in an age of bristling arrogance and dry rationalism. But it was not a weak teaching. The strongest of men is he through whom, because of openness, the Lord can work.

The vernal equinox is now approaching the constellation Aquarius. A more impersonal outlook on the universe is beginning to be felt by many people, a consciousness of abstract, universal law, and a wish to bring all things into harmony with that law. This is a different religious "mood" from that of Pisces. There is less direct concern, now, over what our Heavenly Father may or may not want, personally. The thought is gaining wide acceptance that His pleasure could not be personal at all, but must somehow be related to our own, to *human* welfare. Hence the growing interest in the impersonal vision of Vedanta philosophy, and in the practical techniques of yoga. Yet the Piscean emphasis is not thereby outmoded. Truth is eternal. In each of us, the rays of Pisces operate in varying degrees, making statements of truth with a Piscean slant as valid as any other statement of truth. Jesus' inner vision of reality belongs as truly to Aquarius, or to any other age, as to the age of Pisces.

In this age of growing fascination with an obviously impersonal scheme of things, it would be well for everyone to bear in mind that man's need for love and for empathy with life is not thereby diminished. Nor need the thought of a Universal Consciousness, so popular in religious writing nowadays, banish the thought of an Infinite Being who loves each of us, individually. The concept of infinity must ascribe as much reality to that which is infinitesimal as to vastness or immensity. Life must be *felt;* it is not enough for us merely to cognize it intellectually. The coming Aquarian age should mean, and probably *will* mean, for mankind, not an abandonment of Piscean empathy, but rather the final comprehension and acceptance of what the age of Pisces has tried for so long, and (in its early centuries especially) so unsuccessfully, to teach us.

If your sun is in Pisces, you know, better than the natives of any other sign, that one must flow *with* the tides of life if he would come out on top. What you may still need to learn is which tides to flow with, and which situations to seek as the best ones to come out on top of. Your deep empathy for life can draw you into countless situations, and send you swimming eagerly after numerous goals, that have nothing to do with your own true requirements for spiritual growth.

What you need also is to remember that Piscean empathy is perfected only when it is universalized. That is to say, your feeling for people must be expanded from the few to the many, until it embraces the very universe in your love.

Human giving is usually conditional: Men give so that they may receive something in return. When Jesus said, "It is more blessed to give than to receive" (Acts 20:35), he meant that the feeling of blessedness, or bliss, is its own reward. It is this inner reward, primarily, that should attract your naturally giving nature. Learn to expect nothing in return from the people you love.

Be like the fish that swims out to sea. Surrender your ego and all your desires to the divine; learn to flow effortlessly with the tides of divine grace.

A good meditation for you, as the native of a water sign (and for anyone else for that matter), would be to meditate on water, your "element." In India, certain yogis practice standing in a stream up to their necks, and concentrating on the flowing currents around their bodies. Gradually their minds, too, begin to lose their firm grip on ego, and to flow freely with the currents of life. Other yogis lie on their backs in the water (preferably in *Matsyasana,* the Fish Pose, which you can learn from various books on the yoga postures), and float unresistingly on rising and falling waves. In this way they seek to emphasize in their minds a consciousness of surrender to the waves of divine grace.

Try also sitting very still in meditation. Watch the flow of your thoughts for a time; let your stream of consciousness become ever finer, until no more restless thoughts pass by, polluting its blissful flow.

After some time, allow its waters to reach out in sympathy and love to all humble dwellers in the lowlands of life. Nourish them with your love. Then call them to join you as you flow, with the freedom of perfect self-giving, to merge your little, human feelings in the ocean of infinite Divine Love.

> "When bliss comes over you, you will recognize it as a conscious, intelligent, Universal Being to whom you may appeal, and not as an abstract mental state."
>
> — *Paramhansa Yogananda*

14

Conclusion

Always remember that, while planetary influences ever strike the sounding board of your nervous system, it is a good sounding board, not the vibrations that strike it, that determines the quality of a musical instrument. You cannot change the time you were born, nor the basic planetary pattern that was fixed for you at your birth. This pattern marks what is known in India as your *prarabdha karma*: the experiences that you have to go through as a result of your actions of past lives. You can, however, magnify or minimize those influences, mellow certain of their effects, sharpen others. You can even turn what might have been a harmful influence to good advantage: Perfect the sounding board of a musical instrument, and it will emit a rich tone even if it is struck without feeling.

It may be, according to your *prarabdha karma*, that you were born with an acquisitive nature. You may not be able completely to banish this tendency, and might be working against heavy odds if you tried to do so. You can easily ennoble it, however, by acquiring things for the sole purpose of giving pleasure to others. That, in fact, is what I have tried to do in this book: to help you to work *with* your nature, instead of struggling against it.

It may be according to your "stars," that you are supposed at some time in your life to fall down a staircase and break a leg. Yet you can so strengthen yourself, inwardly, against this karma that all that may happen is that you will trip over the lowest step and bruise a knee. You cannot change the outer astrological influences, but you can do a great deal to change the way you receive them, inwardly.

What I have taught in this book will, I believe, help you in effecting a spiritual change in yourself. For best results, make some use of the suggestions that have been given in *all* of the signs, for though each sign has served as an appropriate doorway through which to introduce a different aspect of spiritual teaching, the teachings themselves are true also generally.

Another way of changing your karma inwardly is more subtle — too subtle, indeed, for presentation in this book. It has to do partly with the ancient and holy science of Kriya Yoga, and partly with the fact that the different planets have their corresponding spiritual centers (or *chakras*) in the body. A knowledge of which planet is weak in one's horoscope, coupled with the deliberate stimulation, or harmonization, of its corresponding center in the body, or of the mental virtues that are associated with that center, can help one to offset that planet's ill effect. I have gone into this subject in some detail in my *Lessons in Yoga: 14 Steps to Higher Awareness* a home-study course, about which you might wish to inquire from the publishers. (A free descriptive brochure can be sent to you.)

Also helpful would be the wearing of certain metals or gems of prescribed weights. Certain pure minerals are believed by yogis to emit powerful beneficial rays that can actually neutralize many of the negative rays of energy afflicting you from without.

Other methods, including ways of strengthening your own magnetic aura so as to neutralize negative outer influences, are taught in my *Lessons in Yoga: 14 Steps to Higher Awareness.* The greatest "technique" of all, however, is to love God and surrender yourself wholly to Him. Remember the words of Jesus: "Seek ye first the kingdom of God, and his righteousness; and all these things shall be added unto you." (Matthew 6:6)

Planetary positions, sun signs, gems and bangles form an interesting enough subject for exploration in their own right. The purpose of this book, however, has not been to fascinate you with an esoteric and remarkable science, but rather to help you to better understand yourself, and (even more important) in the understanding, to improve yourself. May your application of these teachings expand your consciousness, ultimately, to embrace eternity!

WHAT READERS HAVE SAID ABOUT
Your Sun Sign as a Spiritual Guide:

— *"Inspiring"* —

"It's really inspiring to read a book on astrology with such a loving emphasis on the spiritual side."

"I had been an astrologer for seven years when I first came across ***Your Sun Sign as a Spiritual Guide.*** *It elevated my approach to astrology and strengthened and focused my spiritual search."*

— *"Simply and Clearly Written"* —

"The author's words have a down-to-earth, balanced loving quality that reaches the core of my being."

"This book, so beautifully written, with such simplicity and clarity, was just what I needed."

— *"An Aid To Self-Understanding"* —

"This book helped me understand how the universe fits together and how much we are affected by the planets. I liked best the discussion of the spiritual potential of each sun sign, the suggestions for personal growth and pitfalls to watch out for."